Grief Steps®

10 Steps to Rebuild, Regroup and Renew After Any Life Loss

COMPANION WORKBOOK

CHAMPION PRESS LTD.
believing that books can change the world

CHAMPION PRESS, LTD.
FREDONIA, WISCONSIN

Printed in the United States of America
POD 10 9 8 7 6 5 4 3

Dedication

For the beautiful people I met July 9-11, 2003 in Charleston, South Carolina. I dedicate this book in memory of all your children, your siblings and your grandchildren. May you continue to live so fully and courageously in their honor.

ALSO BY BROOK NOEL

Grief Steps®: 10 Steps to Rebuild, Regroup and Renew After Any Life Loss

Surviving Holidays, Birthdays and Anniversaries

Understanding the Emotional and Physical Affects of Grief

The Single Parent Resource

Rituals of Comfort

Back to Basics: 101 Ideas for Strengthening Our Children and Our Families

Shadows of a Vagabond

AUDIO: Now What? Living After Loss

CO-AUTHORED WITH PAMELA D. BLAIR, PH.D.

I Wasn't Ready to Say Goodbye: surviving, coping and healing after the sudden death of a loved One

I Wasn't Ready to Say Goodbye Companion Workbook

You're Not Alone: Resources to Help You Through the Grief Journey

Living with Grief: A Guide to Your First Year of Grieving

My World Is Upside Down: Making Sense of Life After Confronting a Death

Finding Peace: Exercises to Help Heal the Pain of Loss

For more information log onto www.griefsteps.com

"Sorrows are our best educators. [One] can see further through a tear than a telescope."

~ Lord Byron

Contents

An Introduction to Grief Steps®

"What we call the beginning is often the end. To make an end is to make a beginning. The end is where we start from." ~ **T.S. Eliot**

and

There are moments in life where time seems to stand still. Moments where life as we knew it, and life as it will be, collide in tragedy or loss. A valuable relationship may end. We may lose someone we love. We might be fired. An illness or accident may take away functionality that we aren't prepared to lose. A family pet may die. A child may run away, move out or be kidnapped. We might choose or be forced to relinquish an addiction we can't imagine living without. We might be wrapped in depression and unable to "snap out of it." Whatever the trauma, we face that moment of loss with a hurting heart, ill-equipped to handle the impending life change.

Whether our loss is anticipated or sudden, the moment where loss becomes reality leaves our breath caught in our throat, our blood cold, and all we can murmur is… "Why?" Tomorrow loses importance in the face of today's grief, as we wonder how to go on.

These questions have plagued me intensely over the past decade. They plagued me when my perfectly healthy, only sibling was stung by a bee and died within the hour, at age 27. They plagued me when my husband's company gave us three weeks to move across country to a region I had hoped to leave behind forever. They plagued me when my parents divorced and my estranged father continually fell short, offering only false promises. They plagued me when a dear friend was killed in a drunk-driving accident, another lost to leukemia, and yet another to brain cancer.

And, as they plague me, they plague so many others. They plague the many 9/11 survivors I have spoken to and worked with. They plague men and women who have watched their marriages and relationships fail. They plague the parents of children who are diagnosed with unexpected illness. They plague the hearts of pet owners who lose their fury companions. They even plague the person who seems to "have it all," yet feels so empty within. Undeniably, loss becomes just as much a part of life as gain.

At some point we all experience the pain of loss and we each react differently. What one person might consider significant trauma may have little impact on another person. But at some point we will all come face to face with the type of loss that leaves us fumbling and breathless.

The first book I co-authored with Pamela D. Blair on loss, *I Wasn't Ready to Say Goodbye: surviving, coping and healing after the sudden death of a loved one,* is a book I wish I'd never had to author. It was written after the sudden death of my brother. Being a writer, I turned to books for help and was amazed to find that, at the time, there weren't any books dealing specifically with unexpected death. In my brother's honor, I set out to create the most complete book on the topic. With the help of my co-author, I feel we achieved that goal.

That book opened the door to a world I had never expected to enter. It was a world with stories of pain, loss and bittersweet memories. While I had once thought it rare to feel such intense grief, I quickly learned that the world was full of aching hearts behind closed doors. This world contained millions of grievers, who often walked alone, looking for a hand to hold to make it through to another day.

I have learned many valuable lessons in this world of grief. I have also noticed something. After the loss, after the grief work, after the pain, some people readjust and actually live a fuller life. They regroup, re-prioritize, and reconcile themselves to their loss and to their world. They use their pain as a springboard to reach higher ground.

Others do not. Other grievers seem buried beneath their grief, in a constant struggle to find the air to keep them going. The world becomes a dark place with little room for them. Their health declines, and worst of all, their hope declines.

And so the question of "why" surfaced again. This time, I wondered why some people were able to heal and create a springboard from their grief while others wrapped themselves so tightly in their pain they became immobilized.

This phenomenon wasn't just among those who survived the loss of a loved one. The same patterns occurred with those who had lost a valuable relationship, a much-loved pet, a job, a home, a part of themselves.

I set out to answer the following question: What had happened in the lives of those who coped successfully that wasn't happening in the lives of those who couldn't bounce back—even after years had passed? After three years, I began to discover what I now call "Grief Steps®"—actions we must take in order to successfully climb out of the depths of our grief. Although how we each react to our grief is unique, it became apparent that the Steps to escape that darkness are universal. What's more, Grief Steps® can work for any level of loss—whether it be a minor setback or a full-scale catastrophe.

In this book, I aim to share these Grief Steps® with you. They are not rigid concepts, but more of a flowing process. Instead of being ten tidy cups of water, they are like a river, flowing back and forth, slowly then faster, until they lead us to the mouth of the river where life awaits us once again.

While each loss carries unique challenges, this workbook focuses on the universal characteristics of grief. To explore every type of loss would make this book 1000+ pages and leave little of the text relevant to your specific situation. For that reason, I focus on the fundamental, universal Steps we must all take to move successfully through grief.

Despite its pitfalls and potholes, life is a glorious journey. Life is a gift and we are the recipients. As long as it is in our hands, it deserves to be lived. And you deserve the sweetness that comes from living your life fully. May these Steps help you find your way toward that life.

The 10 Grief Steps®

This workbook is organized by order into 10 Grief Steps®. You'll find a chapter devoted to each Step. Here is a summary of the Steps we will take on our journey.

Step One: Shock and Survival
Purpose: To survive the shock of our loss while tending to the basics of reality.

Step Two: The Emotional Rollercoaster
Purpose: To decompress from our shock; and to identify and understand the full range of emotions that accompany our loss.

Step Three: Acknowledgment and Active Grieving
Purpose: To acknowledge the reality of our loss and then acquire the tools and exercises to grieve in a healthy way.

Step Four: Understanding Our Story
Purpose: To find a beginning, middle and end so that we may cease obsessive thinking.

Step Five: Finding Forgiveness
Purpose: To release ourselves from unnecessary pain through the act of forgiveness.

Step Six: Finding Faith
Purpose: To explore, rebuild and repair our faith.

Step Seven: Finding Meaning
Purpose: To understand that even the deepest tragedy can bring meaning, and to uncover that meaning.

Step Eight: Redefining Ourselves
Purpose: To understand the void that has been created by our loss and how that void will change our personal belief system.

Step Nine: Living With Our Loss
Purpose: To integrate our newly discovered meaning into our day-to-day lives and to move forward despite our loss.

Step Ten: Accepting Our New Life
Purpose: To take responsibility that life is ours to be lived to its fullest.

How to Use the Grief Steps® to Get the Most from this Workbook

"we go through the motions until they become real again." ~ **John Steinbeck**

This workbook was created as a proactive tool to accompany the *Grief Steps* book. (Available at your favorite bookstore or at www.griefsteps.com ISBN 1-891400-35-5.) The exercises should be done as you feel comfortable, do not push yourself. Just as there is no timeline to grief, there are no timelines to these exercises. Work through them thoughtfully and slowly—but do work through them. We cannot move forward without action, and this workbook will give you the tools to move forward. Recognize this is a step-by-step process.

There isn't a way to get around the pain that comes with loss. In order to move past it, we must move through it. For that reason, you will be asked to contemplate, ruminate and discover many things about yourself, your loss, and the world we live in. I recommend reading the *Grief Steps* book through first. Then read it a second time with the workbook handy.

The workbook is comprised in the same order as the book. You will find exercises and spaces to explore and record your thoughts and feelings. I also recommend joining the free Grief Steps® support site at www.griefsteps.com. When you join you will receive a Welcome Packet that explains how to use the different areas of the service. Membership includes a 24/7 support message board, twice-monthly chats and a free support newsletter. We also anticipate online support meetings structured specifically around this book. You can learn more about these meetings and other Grief Step® services at the website.

Where Do I Start In My Grief Work?

Much of your grief work will depend on how intricately your loss is woven into your life fabric. Some losses affect only specific areas of our life while leaving other areas unaffected. Other losses seem to touch every part of our being.

When a loss is not completely permeating, it doesn't mean it isn't significant. It simply means that it may require a different series of Grief Steps®. Some of the Steps will be more relevant to your situation, while others will require less time to work through.

When a loss does permeate every fiber of your being, all of the Grief Steps® become necessary for full healing. It is important to pay special attention to the Steps that you want to "skim by" or "ignore." These Steps are often where you need to do the most work.

No matter when your loss occurred, the Grief Steps® can work for you. You may be grieving something that happened days ago or years ago, no matter—unresolved grief does not age. It sits in our souls until we deal with it and work through it. Old wounds and new can be healed through Grief Step work.

I have included a questionnaire on the following pages. You may use it to help you decide which Grief Steps® are most important for your journey. While I recommend reading through the whole book, you don't need to do it in order. This questionnaire is designed to direct you toward the concepts you need to work with the most, or address first. If you have already completed this exercise in the *Grief Steps*® book, save the questionnaire below for six or twelve months down the line—it can serve as a good measure of the progress you will have made.

It is important to pay special attention to Steps that you want to "skim by" or "ignore." These Steps are often where you need to do the most work.

Exploring Grief

This is not a quiz but a questionnaire to help you analyze where to begin your grief work. Grief is not an exact science, so creating a quiz to evaluate where you are in the process would prove extremely challenging. However, the questions on these pages allow you to assess what parts of the grieving process you have completed successfully. Following the questions, you will also find a summary of what your answers mean. Your answers will guide you toward the Steps that will be most helpful to you at this time. Most readers will have two or more Steps they need to work with. When that is the case, begin with the lowest numbered Step and work toward the higher numbered Step. For example, if you found that you scored highest in "Step Five: Finding Forgiveness" and then next in "Step Ten: Accepting Life," begin your grief work with Step Five and then complete Step Ten.

1. My loss occurred within the last 3 months. _____ Y _____ N

2. I feel numb, like I can't believe this has happened. _____ Y _____ N

3. Sometimes I feel like everything is happening in slow motion. _____ Y _____ N

4. If someone asked "How do you feel?" I could identify my emotions. _____ Y _____ N

5. I have felt intense sadness. _____ Y _____ N

6. I have felt intense anger. _____ Y _____ N

7. I understand what happened. _____ Y _____ N

8. My mind is clear and I have quit thinking about this situation
   constantly. _____ Y _____ N

9. I have given myself the time and space to grieve as needed. _____ Y _____ N

10. If the loss occurred over several months ago, I have continued to cry
    occasionally since that time. _____ Y _____ N

11. I talk openly about my loss. _____ Y _____ N

12. Despite my sadness, I have been able to see why the loss
    happened. _____ Y _____ N

13. I have reached out to others in a similar situation and offered my help. _____ Y _____ N

14. I understand what has happened and do not think about my loss
    constantly. _____ Y _____ N

15. I have identified the void left by my loss and have begun to
    take action to fill it. _____ Y _____ N

16. I have continued communicating, in a healthy way, with my friends. _____ Y _____ N

17. I have maintained (or returned to) the hobbies I was engaged in before my loss. ____ Y ____ N

18. I feel bitter inside. ____ Y ____ N

19. I feel angry inside. ____ Y ____ N

If you have a religious background, please answer questions 20-23. If not, please go to question 24.

20. I have quit going to church. ____ Y ____ N
21. I have quit praying. ____ Y ____ N

22. I question how God could let this happen. ____ Y ____ N

23. I don't feel my faith community understands what I am going through. ____ Y ____ N

24. I have created rituals to honor my loss. ____ Y ____ N

25. I can think about my loss without extreme sadness. ____ Y ____ N

26. I am engaging in new hobbies and trying new things. ____ Y ____ N

27. I have made new friends. ____ Y ____ N

28. I have returned to work. ____ Y ____ N

29. I feel hope more often than I feel hopelessness. ____ Y ____ N

30. I see a purpose for my life. ____ Y ____ N

.

> *Grief is never easy... but we need to be easy on ourselves*

Evaluating Your Answers

Questions 1-3

If you answered "yes" to any of these questions, you are likely still experiencing some level of shock. Begin with Step One: Shock and Survival.

Questions 4-6

If you answered "no" to any of these questions, you may not be facing your feelings fully. Work with Step Two: The Emotional Rollercoaster.

Questions 7-8

If you answered "no" to either of these questions, you likely do not understand the story of your loss. Work with Step Four: Understanding Our Story.

Questions 9-11

If you answered "no" to any of these questions, you have probably not grieved as actively as needed or acknowledged your loss completely. Work with Step Three: Acknowledgement and Active Grieving.

Questions 12-13

If you answered "no" to either of these questions, you still need to uncover some meaning behind your loss. Work with Step Seven: Finding Meaning.

Questions 14-17

If you answered "no" to two or more of these questions, you may not have completed the process of redefining yourself and your world. Work with Step Eight: Redefining Ourselves.

Questions 18-19

If you answered "yes" to either of these questions, you may have unresolved forgiveness issues. Work with Step Five: Finding Forgiveness.

Questions 20-23

If you answered "yes" to two or more of these questions, you likely need more support through your faith. Work with Step Six: Finding Faith.

Questions 24-25

If you answered "no" to either of these questions, it is unlikely that you have incorporated your loss into daily living. Please work with Step Nine: Living With Our Loss.

Questions 26-30

If you answered "no" to any of these questions, it is unlikely you have fully accepted life after your loss. Please work with Step Ten: Accepting Our New Life.

Basic Guidelines for Grief Work

Before we begin our journey, I want to outline some basic concepts for our grief work. These are simple reminders for your reference throughout the Grief Steps® process. Read through these periodically, perhaps at the completion of each Step. The statements and the Self-Checks that follow will remind you to be patient and soft with yourself. Grief is never easy, but we need to be easy on ourselves.

I will be patient with myself and understand that grief often involves moving one step forward and two steps back.

I will reach out to others for help when I need support.

I will avoid abusing substances as a way to temporarily minimize my pain.

I will care for myself physically.

I will not isolate myself from friends, hobbies and activities.

I will avoid making major life decisions until I have worked through the Grief Steps®.

I will grieve in my own time and not by how others think I should grieve.

I will create the space and time to honor my emotions.

I will understand that grief recovery takes time, and commit to the Steps—even if relief occurs slower than I would like.

I will remember that moving through grief often involves feeling painful and intense emotions.

I will remember that when I complete my grief work successfully, I can have a rich, although different, life.

Depression and Anxiety

As you work through your grief, it is important to monitor yourself and the stages you are going through. It's important to remember that the psychiatric profession has advanced by leaps and bounds over the past decades. Many doctors are very adept at dealing with emotional and cognitive disorders—from anxiety to depression. Many people have sought professional help with successful results.

> *If you think you might benefit from professional help or medication, at least make an appointment for assessment and learn about your options. Doing so is not a sign of weakness, but a sign of strength. It shows that you are strong enough to deal with your problems—versus brushing them beneath the surface.*

One piece of advice: make sure you feel comfortable with the professional you choose to work with. You should be able to ask questions without feeling rushed. You should feel your questions are answered completely and thoroughly. You should feel that your provider has a genuine interest in what you are saying and is helping you to comprehend and process your grief. If you are the least bit uncomfortable after one or two visits, request a different professional (if others are available at the practice) or call a different service. These are very personal issues that you are dealing with. It is imperative that you feel comfortable, safe and heard. It is not uncommon to go through several providers before you find someone you "connect" with.

> *I will remember that when I complete my grief work successfully,*
> *I can have a rich, although different, life.*

Myth-Breaking: Grief Knows No Timeline

With our world being so orderly and forward-moving, many people who have not experienced grief may pressure you to "get on with life" while your heart and emotions will not cooperate. This push to rejoin life as it once was is unfair and can cause depression and anxiety within. No matter what anyone says, make a pact not to push yourself through the grieving process. Write your name in the blank on the following page.

I, _____, will not allow anyone to push me forward or dictate my timeline for grieving.

I understand that grieving takes time. I am committed to working through my grief, however long it takes. I will not push myself past my means, but I will not use my grief as an excuse to hide from life.

IMPORTANT NOTE: This does not give you permission to hide away and become stagnant. Instead, it gives you permission and time to heal. You may not be ready to put on a cape and jump back into society, but you should not become a statue frozen in time, either. Repeat the following statement aloud:

Healthy Grieving vs. Unhealthy Grieving

In the table on the following page, I have listed examples of healthy and unhealthy grieving. As you work through the Grief Steps®, refer to this chart periodically. Note which statements describe you. If you repeatedly find yourself grieving in unhealthy ways, seek the help of a support group or professional for guidance in your grief work.

Healthy Grieving	Unhealthy Grieving
Although saddened, you communicate honestly with friends and family.	☐ Avoiding friends and family for a prolonged period of time (over three weeks).
You tend to your basic self-case needs.	You are not eating well, sleeping well or tending to your basic self-care needs.
You have accepted the reality of your loss.	You are in denial about your loss or still trying to "go back in time" and change the outcome.
Although you may occasionally have a self-destructive thought, it passes quickly and the majority of your focus is on moving forward.	You have persistent, obsessive or strong self-destructive thoughts. (Seek help immediately.)
You have discovered healthy outlets for your anger.	You take your anger out on yourself or those people close to you. (Seek help immediately.)
You realize that your world has changed and are sad about this change, but are open to what it may bring.	You have become immobilize by depression and cannot see hope for the future. (Seek help immediately.)
You are facing your feelings.	You are masking your feelings through self-medication.

Step One: Shock and Survival

Purpose: To survive the shock of our loss, while tending to the basics of reality.

◆

"And people cooked for me.
And people answered the phone for me.
People cared for me when I didn't care."
~ **Wendy Feiereisen**

When faced with grief, our bodies and minds tend to shut down. The reason is quite simple. Since we are almost always ill-prepared to handle loss, our body seeks to protect itself by shutting down the senses. This allows the body to "tune out" the pain. This "tuning out" accounts for many of the ways grievers describe this initial stage...

I felt like I was in a movie.
The world seemed dreamlike.
Everything seemed to move in slow motion.
I felt complete numbness.
I felt catatonic.
I went crazy—like an animal.

As you recall your own initial grief and shock, how would you describe them?

_____

_____

_____

_____

_____

All of these statements and emotions are normal. They all express different ways that our body filters information—letting just select facts into our consciousness.

When we understand the first emotions that have filtered through, our bodies let more emotion through. The process continues until we can fully comprehend and prepare to face our loss. This is the "acute" stage of shock. Like you will see in many other areas of grief, there is no exact timetable or schedule. We all grieve in our own way and in our own time.

The intensity of our loss often influences our level of shock. If we are facing a loss where we had time to prepare, the shock phase may be shorter. When the loss is very sudden, it tends to take longer to loosen shock's grip. The shock phase can last anywhere from several days to several months. If you find yourself still in "acute" shock (acute shock can be defined by an inability to accept reality or function in reality) after six weeks, it may be a sign that professional help is needed. After six weeks, you should be able to see clear signs of progress. You are probably far from "okay" but you have:

1. Identified and begun to understand what has happened.
2. Accepted the loss as reality.
3. Started grieving for the loss in a healthy way.

Explore where you are in this initial stage of grieving by answering the following questions.

1. What are you grieving?

_____
_____
_____
_____
_____
_____
_____
_____
_____

2. Do you understand the finality of this loss?

_____
_____
_____
_____
_____

3. For each of the two statements below, circle which one most describes you.

Healthy Grieving	Unhealthy Grieving
Although saddened, you communicate honestly with friends and family.	Avoiding friends and family for a prolonged period of time (over three weeks).
You tend to your basic self-case needs.	You are not eating well, sleeping well or tending to your basic self-care needs.
You have accepted the reality of your loss.	You are in denial about your loss or still trying to "go back in time" and change the outcome.
Although you may occasionally have a self-destructive thought, it passes quickly and the majority of your focus is on moving forward.	You have persistent, obsessive or strong self-destructive thoughts. (Seek help immediately.)
You have discovered healthy outlets for your anger.	You take your anger out on yourself or those people close to you. (Seek help immediately.)
You realize that your world has changed and are sad about this change, but are open to what it may bring.	You have become immobilize by depression and cannot see hope for the future. (Seek help immediately.)
You are facing your feelings.	You are masking your feelings through self-medication.

Analyzing Your Answers

If your answer to question one is short or vague, you are either moving through the exercise too quickly, or you have not come to terms with this initial stage and step. Until you can fully and honestly expose what you are grieving, you cannot take steps to move forward. I would recommend working through Step Two, and then coming back and trying to answer question one again. Also, make sure you have read the entire *Grief Steps* book. When you have completed those two tasks, you will likely be able to answer this question more thoroughly. If, at that point, you still cannot answer thoroughly, you may need some help to get through the initial shock. Consider a support group, trusted friend or professional to help you absorb the reality of your experience.

If your answer to question two is "no," "sort of," or anything other than "yes," please re-read the above paragraph, as that same tactic should be applied.

If you circled more than two statements in the unhealthy column, or you circled numbers the unhealthy answer in questions 3, 4 or 5, you should seek help through a support group or professional.

If you were able to answer question one thoroughly, answered yes to question two, and had two or less circles in the unhealthy grieving quiz, you have taken great strides toward moving through this initial phase. Continue in this chapter. While you may feel you are moving into a darker place, indeed you are moving forward.

A Note about Substance Abuse

It is important to note the temptation to abuse substances to null the pain of grief. While they can offer a temporary escape, they will not move you past the pain. Instead, they act like a "pause button." Substances seem to stop grief in its tracks, but don't be fooled, grief waits for you.

At this stage, we are extremely vulnerable. It is easy to fall into an addiction, especially when it seems to make our pain easier to withstand. But we aren't solving anything. We are simply delaying our recovery. We are also compounding it, since at some point we will have to deal with our addiction—and our grief will be waiting for us too.

If you sense yourself getting caught up in a vice to deal with your sadness, seek professional help or a support group.

Be cautious about the use of medication or substances to help you through grief. Remember that there is no way to move around grief, we must move through it. Self-medication only delays that process

What to Expect: Physical and Emotional Changes

Fear and anxiety increase when we face the unknown. When we understand that we are traveling a path others have traveled and survived, our fear and anxiety often lessen. Below, I have listed common physical and emotional affects encountered within the grief journey. You may experience some or all of these affects. When you feel them, realize they are normal. You are not going crazy. You are not alone. This is part of the process. Instead of worrying or obsessing about these "side affects" focus your energy on the "Three Goals for the First Few Weeks" (that are covered in the following pages):

Chest pain	Restlessness	Sleep difficulties
Dry mouth	Crying	Exhaustion
Weakness	Dizziness	Numbness
Shakiness	Disorientation	Listlessness
Migraines or headaches	Upset stomach	Heart palpitations
Anxiety	Poor appetite	Overeating
Social avoidance	Shortness of breath	Aches and Pains

Three Goals for the First Few Weeks

As we move through Step One, I want to encourage you to focus on three goals:

1. Absorb shock and identify your emotions
2. Seek support in daily living
3. Express your feelings and emotions

GOAL ONE:

Absorbing Shock and Identifying Our Emotions

We need to give ourselves time and space for reality to soak in. We need a place where we feel safe to express our emotions. When we need to cry, yell, rant or rave, we need to honor those feelings and have the space to do so. Often, we don't take the time to *truly feel* our emotions. We get so caught up in society's stereotyping—"Just move on," "It's not safe/acceptable to reveal your emotions, "You're making too much out of this,"—that we repress our feelings. They become buried in our souls and stay there until we go back, dig them up, and work through them (a process we discuss in detail in Step Three).

To complicate matters, we cannot put life on hold while we deal with the acute pain of our loss. No matter what we have gone through there are still bills to be paid, children to raise, household duties and obligations. Somehow we have to continue the motions of living.

The use of Grief Sessions can be helpful as look for healthy ways to cope. "Grief Sessions" are basically "scheduled" times to experience emotions. It can be helpful to set up Grief Sessions for yourself in these first few weeks. Find a place where you feel safe to let go. Then visit that place twenty minutes each day to get in touch with, and experience, your feelings.

Where can you go, where you will be undisturbed for twenty minutes each day? Could you take a walk? Drive to a park? Go in your room? Where do you feel safe to "let go?"

_____

_____

_____

Can you spend twenty minutes there today—and each day as you work through your grief? Write it on your calendar. Write down below when you will go.

_____

_____

_____

Keep in mind that Goal One doesn't involve trying to change your emotions or work through them. Goal One is simply concerned with *feeling* your emotions—whatever they may be.

Find a place where you feel safe to release your feelings and emotions. Try to do this for 20 minutes each day.

GOAL TWO: Seek Support for Daily Living

Continuing through the motions of living brings us to the second goal—support. Make a list of the commitments you must keep. A worksheet is provided in this chapter. (If you are in a severe state of disorganization, have a close friend help you with your list.)

Make a list of people who would be willing to help you keep your commitments. These may be friends who have already offered assistance or those in your community you feel comfortable asking for help. Try to delegate as many of the "daily living" tasks as possible during the first few weeks of acute grief. This will give you more time and energy, for honoring your emotions and to begin the healing process.

Reaching out isn't easy, but it is necessary.

GOAL THREE: Express Your Emotions

In Goal One we work toward *feeling* our emotions. We give them space to take on a life of their own instead of suppressing them. Goal Three involves taking the emotions we feel and finding a way to express them outwardly as a step toward healing. Although they sound similar, both of these steps are very different and both are needed for healing.

The first goal requires us to get in touch with what we feel and to let it flow through us. In Goal Three, we actively search to understand these emotions, and to make sure we are handling them in a healthy way. For example, you can know that you are angry but choose not to do anything about it. Goal Three requires that we identify our emotions, such as the anger in the example, and then actively make healthy choices about them. We don't let our emotions fester internally causing unneeded physical and emotional turmoil. Instead, we choose to acknowledge the variety of emotions we are feeling and handle them healthily. There are many ways to express our emotions in the next chapter of this workbook.

Understanding Our Support Needs

Reaching out to others for help is difficult, especially when we are at an emotional low and our energy is at a premium. Yet, it remains vital to identify the support that we need in our lives. In the chart below, write down each specific support need in the first column. In the next column, write down who can give you that support. Once you have completed your chart, make an action plan to contact the people in column two to get the support that will help you heal.

WHAT TYPE OF SUPPORT I NEED	WHO CAN GIVE ME THAT SUPPORT
Talking / Communication	
Physical tasks / Self-Care	
Financial Needs	
Day-to-day Life management	
Professional or group support	

What If I'm Past the Acute Grief Stage?

If you are coming to this book several months or even several years after your loss, you may well be beyond the focus of Step One. You might read Step One and think—"I didn't do those things—what now?" Don't worry. While you may not have accepted and felt your emotions as thoroughly as you would have had you completed this workbook, there are still plenty of ways to unfold the past so that you can face it successfully and move forward with your grief work. No matter when we experience our grief, if we have not dealt with it thoroughly, it remains in wait. There will be exercises to help you recall past, unresolved grief in Step Three.

Even before exploring Step Three, I do recommend that you begin keeping a journal. This journal will become a very valuable tool as you work through your Steps. I recommend journaling at least two pages each night before going to bed. Write down whatever comes to mind. If you are having problems getting started, see the ideas and starters within this chapter or simply begin with the words... "I feel..." Each time you get stuck, go back and begin again with, "I feel..." It doesn't matter if the writing is grammatically correct or poetic—all that matters is that you are getting your emotions down on paper and expressing them outwardly. Through doing this, we take emotions that we may have hidden or suppressed and move them outside of ourselves to where we can deal with them effectively.

If you are not a writer, try keeping a "Voice Journal" by speaking into a tape recorder. It doesn't matter what method you use, but it is important to release the emotions through voice or writing. Take the emotions from being internal thoughts to giving them physical form. Once we have identified and put our emotions into a physical form, we will be able to better understand our feelings and consequently work through them—our goal to becoming healthy.

> *Choose some form of journaling, whether written or voice, and begin using it daily to release emotions.*

Step One often feels like a slippery ice rink where we are without skates. We are barraged with feelings and challenges at a time when our emotional and physical energy are at a premium. It is important to be easy with yourself, and reduce stress and expectations as much as possible during this period. Taking this time to identify and experience your emotions (to their fullest) will help you immensely as you move forward down grief's pathway.

Self-Check

As you work through your grief, it's important to monitor yourself during these stages. The following list can help you discern healthy grief from distorted grief. If you feel you may be suffering unhealthy grief, seek the help of a support group, clergy person or therapist.

Check any unhealthy stages you are experiencing.

☐ Extreme Avoidant Behavior – If you are avoiding friends and family for a prolonged period of time (over three weeks) you will want to talk to a professional. People need each other to work through grief.

☐ Lack of Self-Care – In order to have the energy and emotional capacity to work through grief, one must first take care of his/her basic needs. If you are having problems meeting basic needs, this is a warning sign to seek help. (A 24 to 72 hour-bout of decreased self-care is normal. If you cannot take care of your most basic needs—food, sleep, showering, etc.—seek outside assistance.)

☐ Prolonged Denial – If months have passed and you are still in denial, you will most likely need a support group to help you move through this stage.

☐ Self-Destructive Thoughts – These thoughts are not unusual during the initial shock of grief, but we can expect them to pass quickly. If they are persistent or obsessive it is best to consult a professional for guidance in working through them. If any of these thoughts involve serious harm to yourself (or someone else) seek help immediately.

☐ Displaced Anger – With few emotional outlets available to us, it is common for anger to be displaced. However, this can become problematic if your anger is hurting you in personal or professional areas, or hurting others—seek help immediately.

☐ Prolonged Depression or Anxiety – Like denial, prolonged and immobilizing depression, or debilitating anxiety are signs to seek professional help.

☐ Self-Medication – If you are using substances in excess to self-medicate your pain, i.e. food, alcohol or drugs, seek the help of an organization that specializes in such disorders, or the help of a professional.

☐ Revenge or retribution – If you are preoccupied with revenge or retribution toward someone affiliated with your loss, seek immediate help. This is a very dangerous deversion that cannot be taken lightly.

Notes:

Step Two:
The Emotional Rollercoaster

Purpose: To decompress from our shock and to identify and understand the full range of emotions that accompany our loss.

◆

"Problems do not go away. They must be worked through or else they remain, forever a barrier to the growth and development of the spirit." ~ **M. Scott Peck**

The second Grief Step® involves identifying, understanding and facing our emotions. In order to move through our grief, we must face it head on. Often at the time of loss, we are simply incapable of comprehending or coping with our emotions. Then, as life beckons, we push our feelings aside or bury them within. Days, months and sometimes years drift by. We feel a gnawing sadness, but aren't sure of its source—or what to do about it. We know it is dark and ugly so we try to avoid it—often staying as far away from our emotions as possible. Some of us are scared that if we dig into that darkness, we might never come out.

Ironically, we should be just as afraid of what happens when we don't dig into that darkness. When we leave it there to fester, it becomes the budding ground for our future. Everything we experience must filter through that dark pile before blossoming.

The process is somewhat like a root canal. We don't want to experience the pain of the root canal, but we don't want to experience the continuing pain of the toothache, either. The only way to obtain lasting comfort is by undergoing the pain of the root canal. To get past the pain, we must move through it. There simply isn't any other way.

For some, this process moves relatively quickly. It's as if a dam has burst and long-suppressed emotions flood forth. For others, the process may require a chisel, to chip away at the wall built within.

As you explore your emotions you may find the help of a support group or a professional extremely valuable. Or you may choose a close friend, pastor, or online support site such as www.griefsteps.com, to share your excavating process. And by all means, if at any point you fear you might inflict harm on yourself or others, seek professional help immediately.

I have always had a difficult time expressing my emotions. I can write about other peoples' feelings, expressing concepts on paper—but when it comes to verbalizing my own feelings, I often can't find the words. I remember one particular therapist's frustration peaking when he asked me for the fifth time, "How do you feel?" My response was the same as my first four, "I don't know!" What I learned was that "I don't know" often equals "I don't want to know."

We may not want to know what we feel because it scares us. We may not want to know how we feel because then we are responsible for doing something about it.

I am an upbeat and optimistic person. I didn't want to feel the sadness of my loss. I felt it would reduce my productivity and affect how I cared for my family. I didn't want people to see me sad. I didn't want anyone to see me weak. But when it comes to grief, avoidance is never bliss. There cannot be bliss again until we have dug out of the darkness.

Later, we will look at some specific tools to use when facing your emotions. For now, let's look at the different emotions that often travel with grief.

When we answer the question, "How do I feel?" with "I don't know," it may mean "I don't want to know." Owning our emotions requires us to take responsibility. This responsibility is the only way to move forward into healing.

Feeling Practice

Learning to identify our emotions is half the battle. We often get so caught up in describing our environment, our pain, or our busyness that we cannot label the internal emotion. Ask yourself "How do I feel right now?" Record the answer below. Continue to do this periodically (at least three times a week) to practice getting in touch with your feelings.

_____

_____

_____

Exploring Emotions

Anger...read pages 55-58 of the *Grief Steps*® book before completing this exercise.

Of all the emotions, anger is the most difficult to deal with. We live in a society where anger is frowned upon. Anger scares people. Anger indicates that we are "out of control." Angry people are often labeled "bad people." However there is a big difference between an angry person and a person who is "feeling" their anger. The latter is a temporary state—not a permanent one. But, when we don't allow our anger the opportunity to pass through us, it takes hold and we experience life through an angry lens of distortion. We might be outwardly angry and loud—or we may be quietly angry. We look happy and nice most of the time—but then we give someone a little jab here or a little jab there. Or we might become bitter, which is the debilitating cousin to anger (see pages 60-62 in the Grief Steps® book).

The question becomes: how do we honor and feel our anger in a world where anger is considered "bad"? We accept that anger is not bad—only staying angry is. We must learn to accept that by feeling our anger and allowing it to pass, we are letting it go instead of letting it take root. We must learn to make space to honor our emotions—the good, the bad and the ugly, with the hope of moving forward. On the following pages you will find several worksheets to help you explore and handle angry feelings.

Why Am I Angry?

Our anger often stems from feeling something unjust or preventative has occurred. We might feel that we could have done something differently, and thus direct our anger inward. Or, we might feel that those around us should have done something differently and direct our anger outward.

What "should haves" and "could haves" do you recite repeatedly to yourself? Include those you feel you personally "should have done" as well as the "should haves" and "could haves" for other people involved in your loss. IMPORTANT: Don't censor your list. If you feel angry about something yet don't want to write it down because it "doesn't make sense" or is "ridiculous"—that is all the more reason to write it down. We must get our feelings out-in-the-open in order to deal with them. Try this now by completing the sentences below.

I am angry because I think I (could/should) have...	*I am angry because I think _____ (could/should) have...*

Understanding Anger and Finding Support

Anger also occurs when we suppress our feelings. Anger is not the most accepted emotion in today's culture. In fact, some people don't even recognize anger as part of the grieving process. Depending on our support network and situation, we may be encouraged not to show our anger. When this happens, the anger still exists and needs to be released, so it is released inward, usually causing corresponding guilt. This can cause a variety of problems. We may become sick, depressed, have chronic pain or begin having nightmares. Discovering healthy ways to release our anger and curb our guilt are important for healing.

What have you been taught about anger?

_____

_____

_____

_____

_____

_____

Who around you does not accept your anger?

_____

_____

_____

Who around you can handle your anger?

_____

_____

_____

What can you do to spend more time around those who can handle your emotions and less time around those people that won't? If you don't have a support person (or people) who can handle your anger…what steps might you take to create that? (Could you contact a professional, join a group, etc.)

_____

_____

_____

_____

_____

Appropriate Anger

Appropriate anger is the point to which we all hope to get eventually. In this phase we can take our anger, in whatever form, and vent it. There are many ways to release anger appropriately. Place a checkmark next to any of the ideas below that you think would be helpful to you. Try one of these exercises the next time you find yourself upset and anger-ridden.

- ☐ Beat a pillow.
- ☐ Create a sacred space where you can go to not be heard or seen, to let the anger out of your system.
- ☐ Use journaling to record and release your angry feelings.
- ☐ Accept that anger is not bad—only staying angry is. We learn to accept that fact by feeling our anger and allowing it to pass, instead of taking root.
- ☐ Take a walk out into an unpopulated area and scream until you are exhausted.
- ☐ Talk with a friend, therapist or counselor.
- ☐ Have a good cry, let the tears flow.

What other ideas can you think of to deal with anger? Try to come up with at least three.

_____

_____

_____

_____

_____

_____

_____

_____

_____

Practice being Angry

Because society may have taught us that anger is not acceptable, we may have a hard time expressing and venting our emotions. If this describes your situation, allow yourself to "practice being angry." It might sound crazy at first, but think about it—if you don't get the emotion out it is going to stay wedged within you. There is nothing pretty about anger. Schedule an hour a week and "let it out" using one of the methods you learned about in this section. Next week, try a different technique. Keep using these techniques until you can feel the anger lift. Write down a schedule for these "practice" sessions.

Anxiety

Anxiety…read pages 59-60 of the *Grief Steps*® book before completing this exercise.

Anxiety is a sense of nervousness, edginess or agitation, often without a readily identifiable source. Sometimes anxiety is attached to an event that we consider difficult or dangerous, like driving in a strange city, or facing an unknown future. We feel our heart race, our palms sweat and a general sense of unease. At its worst, anxiety turns into a panic attack where our breathing is stifled and we may feel like we are having a heart attack.

Anxiety is often accompanied by additional emotions—fear, anger, sadness—it tends to travel with a partner. When we feel anxious, the most important thing we can do is pinpoint the cause, take a deep breath and conduct a "reality check" using the questions below.

What do I feel anxious about?

_____

_____

_____

Now, take a few minutes and just sit still. Do nothing. Then ask and answer the question again.

_____

_____

_____

Repeat this one more time. Sit still for several minutes and then write another answer.

_____

_____

_____

Your answer most likely developed or changed each time you asked yourself the question. If not, continue asking yourself this question until you find an answer that carries some "zing" to it. You'll know in your gut when you have stumbled on the true source of your anxiety. Often, you'll have to ask yourself this question several times to get to the true source.

Once you have uncovered the true source, write it down at the top of the following page, rewording it one more time.

Analyzing Anxiety

I feel anxious about _____

_____

_____

Now, let's explore "fact and fiction" as it correlates to your statement. In the "fact" boxes, record every fact you have experienced or know, that supports your anxious position. In the "fiction" column, record each experience that refutes your statement.

For example, if you have written, "I feel anxious about driving in a big city because I think I will get into an accident," write down what reality supports your statement and what doesn't. If you have driven in the city before, and were not in an accident, that would be a strike against your anxiety. If you took your time, wore your seat-belt and had a good map, those would be a few more strikes against your anxiety. Continue looking for "faults" in your anxiety. This exercise can often decrease or eliminate our anxiety altogether.

Fact	Fiction

As unfair and as unjust as life can be, it always offers us a choice. Remember that 98% of what we worry about never happens. Living in a state of perpetual worry is a terrible way to live life. If you find yourself constantly riddled by anxiety, you will need an arsenal of cognitive exercises (like the aforementioned "Reality Check") to begin to loosen anxiety's hold. You may also want to consult a professional to see if you have General Anxiety Disorder. This disorder is quite prevalent in today's hectic world and there are supportive systems in place to help those who are suffering in its grip.

Anxiety Screening

General Anxiety Disorder (GAD) is a serious medical illness that affects approximately four million Americans every year. It is twice as likely to affect women. While only a professional can make a thorough screening and active diagnosis, the following questions can help you determine if GAD is affecting your life and you should consult a professional. Keep in mind that GAD can be treated, so if these symptoms resonate with you, help is as close as your phone book. Call a Psychiatrist and let them know that you believe you have GAD and would like to be seen for a complete diagnosis.

Yes No   Do you suffer from excessive worrying?
Yes No   Do you have difficulty controlling your worrying?
Yes No   Has this persistent worrying lasted for at least six months?

If the answer to any of the above questions is YES, then continue to answer the questions below.

Have you been bothered by any of the following for at least six months?

Yes No   Restlessness, feeling keyed-up or on edge?
Yes No   Being easily tired?
Yes No   Problems concentrating?
Yes No   Irritability?
Yes No   Muscle tension?
Yes No   Trouble falling asleep or staying asleep, or restless and unsatisfying sleep?
Yes No   Anxiety interfering with your daily life?

If you answered "Yes" to at least three of these 6 questions, you may well be suffering from GAD. Call a psychiatrist as mentioned above for a complete diagnosis.

Adapted from:
Diagnostic and Statistical Manual of Mental Disorders, Fourth Edition. Washington, DC: American Psychiatric Association, 1994.

The Blame Game

Blame is dangerous. When we sit with blame, we give ourselves an excuse not to move forward. Everything is someone else's fault. Our pain, our sadness, our depression—it's all someone else's doing.

"If only" are two words uttered over and over again when we are stuck in the blame game. Instead of moving forward, we recount the ways our life could be different "if only" something would or wouldn't have happened. Blame becomes anger's "scapegoat."

Blame is a mask. When you take it off, you often see fear. Fear to feel our emotions, fear to go inside and dig through the darkness. Or you may see anger and unforgiveness. When we feel angry we don't have to think ahead toward hope. We don't have to plan for the future—because our future remains at the hands of someone or something else.

Through blame, we can seemingly skip the parts of life we don't want to face and page forward to something else. Or we can page backward and recant the "if only's" of a past we cannot change.

When we get stuck in the blame game we halt our grief work. We can attempt to move forward but the game will always be waiting for us. Moving through blame is much like moving through anxiety.

First, write down who you blame and for what. Sometimes we blame ourselves. No matter whom or what it is, write it down. Use the space below to write down who you blame in your life for your misfortune, unhappiness or whatever other difficult emotion you are experiencing.

_____

_____

_____

_____

_____

_____

_____

_____

_____

_____

Now let's examine the evidence you have to support your claim. This will allow you to quickly see whether your blame is founded or unfounded. If we find that reality does not support our blame, we can then begin to let that blame go. Each time we repeat the feeling we can dig for another fact that demonstrates its untruth.

Analyzing Blame

(See the instructions on the proceeding page.)

Who do I blame and why?	
Evidence to support	Evidence to refute

When Blame has Merit

Sometimes, our blame is justified. For example, perhaps someone we loved developed lung cancer because they smoked cigarettes. We may blame them for the illness. Or, perhaps someone we loved was killed in a drunk driving accident. We may blame the person who drank. These cases have a solid argument for blame. In these cases, we need to move toward forgiveness (which we cover in detail in Step Five.) Blame, like guilt, doesn't hurt anyone but the beholder. By choosing to hold onto blame you are tightening its grip on your life. Sometimes, ironically, detachment takes the form of attachment to something else. In order to detach from our feelings and our pain, we attach ourselves to work, to a hobby, or to a substance. We find something to occupy us other than the pain we feel inside, providing a way to avoid, rather than address, forgiveness.

What blame are you experiencing that has merit?

_____

_____

_____

_____

_____

What do you gain by holding onto this blame?

_____

_____

_____

_____

How does this blaming-process hurt you?

_____

_____

_____

_____

_____

_____

How would your life be different if you could forgive and let go?

_____

_____

_____

Bitterness

Bitterness is born from an incomplete grieving cycle. Somewhere within the process of grieving we chose to stand still instead of move forward. Read pages 60-61 of the Grief Steps book and then review the Grief Steps on pages 22-24. If you are experiencing bitterness, use the space below to write about feelings of unresolved grief, and where and when you may have "halted" your grieving cycle.

_____

_____

_____

_____

_____

_____

_____

_____

_____

_____

_____

_____

_____

_____

_____

_____

_____

_____

_____

_____

_____

_____

_____

_____

_____

_____

_____

_____

_____

_____

Detachment

Often, when we experience the initial shock of our loss, we temporarily detach from the world around us. It is too hard to face our loss, so our body shuts down, blocking out reality. If we move through our grief work successfully, little by little we reopen ourselves to reality until we fully rejoin society. When we don't successfully complete our grief work, we remain in a state of detachment where we continue to withdraw from people, hobbies, events and feelings.

How can you tell if you are in a state of detachment? Begin by answering the questions below.

1. What activities have you quit participating in since your grief began (if any)?

_____

_____

_____

2. What people have you quit spending time with since your grief began (if any)?

_____

_____

_____

3. What activities did you do in your "private time" (read, exercise, craft, play music) that you have quit doing (if any)?

_____

_____

_____

4. How do you feel right now?

_____

_____

_____

Looking at how you answered questions 1-3, write about the positive or negative influence these actions have had on your life in the space below.

_____

_____

_____

Analyzing Your Answers

When you evaluated how your answers to statements one through three affected your life, what did you discover? Did you find that you have made positive choices, letting go of people that were hurtful or activities that took away from your priorities? Or is the contrary true? Have you removed yourself from activities and people that are beneficial to you? If you have done the latter, you are in the process of detachment.

When you answered question four—were you able to identify how you feel—or were you at a loss for words, stumbling to get a sentence down? If you had trouble articulating your feelings, you are likely in a state of detachment.

Detachment is a seemingly productive amour we wear when we are hurt. Theoretically it seems like a good approach—place a shield around ourselves to prevent further hurt. However, the exact opposite ultimately happens. Instead of blocking further hurt, we create a shield that holds our hurts and painful experiences within us. Our bodies become a prison. When we realize there can be no love without pain, no happiness without sadness, we realize that we must remove this shield in order to move toward happiness once again.

Reviewing how you answered the questions on the previous page, what steps can you take (little steps) to move toward the healthy things that you have detached from? List as many as you can think of below. Then choose one of your ideas that you can implement in the next 10 days. Once completed, come back and choose another. Continue this process until you feel the shield around you dissolving.

_____
_____
_____
_____
_____
_____
_____
_____
_____
_____
_____
_____
_____

Guilt

Of all the blocks mentioned, guilt may be the strongest of all. Struggling with the question, "Why did this happen to me?" can create so much anxiety, pain and self-doubt that you stay stuck in your grief, much longer and more intensely than needed.

The causes of guilt are varied depending on the type of loss we have experienced. If we are the family breadwinner and lose our job, we may feel intense guilt about "letting our family down." We may feel that guilt is the way to "pay penance" or that intense guilt is required because of our loss.

However, we must remember that guilt is a useless emotion. It's like a glue that cements us to our pain. We cannot move forward when shrouded with guilt. We must remind ourselves that our goal is to overcome this negative feeling and resume a healthy lifestyle full of meaning. Harboring guilt won't let us do that.

Process your guilt with a trusted friend, therapist, clergy person or through the exercise found below.

Below, write at least a one-page letter to the person or situation you are grieving. Tell them whatever you want but remember to include the following:

- the facts of what happened
- how you feel about what happened
- how this loss has affected your life

Now, turn the page over and imagine the deceased responding to your letter. Asking questions of the deceased will make this exercise extremely valuable. So write down such questions as, "How do you feel about what happened?" and "Will you please forgive me for _____?" "Have I been punished enough for my part (real or imagined) in all of this and is there anything else I can do to show you how sorry I am?" "How can I show you how much I have suffered?" Then close your eyes and answer each question as if they were speaking through you.

If you find this is a difficult exercise to do on your own you may want to ask a therapist or trusted friend to sit quietly with you. **Caution:** If you are being "told" by your inner voice to hurt yourself in any way, seek professional help immediately.

Use the space on the following page to write the letter.

Now write back to yourself, imagining how this person or situation would respond.

_____
_____
_____
_____
_____
_____
_____
_____
_____
_____
_____
_____
_____
_____
_____
_____
_____
_____
_____
_____
_____
_____
_____
_____
_____
_____
_____
_____
_____
_____
_____
_____
_____
_____

(Exercise adapted from I Wasn't Ready to Say Goodbye: surviving, coping and healing after the sudden death of a loved one by Brook Noel and Pamela D. Blair, Ph.D. ISBN 1-891400-27-4, Published by Champion Press, Ltd.)

Self-Loathing

It's important to check for self-hatred or self-loathing. Often, self-loathing isn't obvious, but look a little deeper. Are you engaging in any activities that are causing you harm? Do you drink excessively, overeat (or under-eat), smoke, abuse prescription or non-prescription drugs?

What exists in your life that may be a symptom of self-loathing?

_____

_____

_____

_____

Think of someone you love dearly. Would you ever knowingly hurt them? Would you try to help them if you felt they were drinking excessively, using food as a vice, abusing prescription or non-prescription medicines? If they constantly belittled themselves or threatened to harm themselves would you step in? What if they tried to "shut themselves off" from the world at large? As a true friend, you would likely try to help. We do not unknowingly let our friends go through pain. Likewise, we need to have that same love for ourselves—stepping in when we see our own self-hatred causing pain or deterioration.

When you are in a dark place, what negative messages do you tell yourself? (Do you tell yourself you are unworthy, destined to be unhappy, a 'bad person'?)

_____

_____

_____

_____

Now imagine a close friend coming to you and expressing the feelings you recorded in the last question. What would you say to him or her?

_____

_____

_____

_____

_____

_____

_____

_____

Look at how you answered the two proceeding questions. What is the difference between how you treat yourself and how you would treat a close friend? Write yourself a note, applying the same tender touch you used with your close friend.

_____

_____

_____

_____

_____

_____

_____

_____

_____

_____

_____

_____

_____

_____

When we are able to see these excesses and abuses they become signals that there is some degree of self-hatred within us. These abuses are quite common. I know I have had my share of them. These abuses are clues that we have not found the wholeness, meaning and peace that we deserve to find in this lifetime. They are also signals that we are on the wrong path. Instead of looking within, we have looked to our excesses for the peace we haven't found within ourselves.

So where does this self-hatred or self-destructiveness stem from? Why do we engage in these excesses to begin with? It is all tied back to our feelings. We tend to live much of our life on autopilot, not in tune with our feelings from moment-to-moment. When we find ourselves with feelings of anger or sadness or depression we don't know what to do. We know we don't have the skills to cope (or at least we don't think we do). And besides, dealing with these emotions seems so "messy." Why do that, when we live in a world of instant gratification? Why go through months of grief work when we can reach for a pill or a drink or a chocolate to seemingly alleviate the pain? Instead of developing that arsenal of emotional skills to deal with our feelings, we develop an arsenal of excesses to cover them up. We pile bandage upon bandage until we forget how the original wound was caused in the first place.

What bandages have you used to cover your symptoms of emotional distress?

_____

_____

_____

_____

How have those bandages helped or hindered you?

_____

_____

_____

_____

_____

_____

_____

The process of overcoming our excesses and healing our self-hatred involves pealing back the bandages, one by one, until we expose the original wound. Then we heal the original wound. As we learn to understand, express and honor our feelings the wound begins to heal. As it does, the excesses become unneeded and begin to fall away on their own.

Helplessness

Helplessness stems from not knowing our own power. When we underestimate or are detached from the miracles that we are, and the power we can exert, we feel helpless. We feel our lives moving forward and that we have little control over the process. We no longer know how to cope or make decisions. We don't know how to get from Point A to Point B—sometimes we don't even know where Point A or Point B are.

Helplessness can also come from being stifled when life seems to pile one thing then another on top of us. The bigger the pile the more overwhelmed we become until our overwhelmed feelings transform to helplessness. The pile is so big, we don't know where to start. And so we don't. As we remain inactive, the pile gets bigger, further propelling our sense of helplessness.

What pressures, emotions, and internal or external things are weighing on you today?

_____

_____

_____

_____

_____

_____

The way out of this vicious cycle begins by realizing that we do have a choice. We always have a choice. The journey begins the day we make the choice to take the first Step. Keep in mind I wrote *step* not *leap*. We take one little step at a time, honing our skills, until we emerge from our sense of helplessness. What is one step you can take to deal with one simple aspect of the pressures you listed above? What is one thing you can do today to begin to realize you are not helpless—you do have control.

_____

_____

_____

_____

The Steps within this workbook can carry you through unresolved grief and show you the way out of this dark place. Take a little step... then another... then another... Yes, grief is a journey of 2000 miles, but as the Chinese proverb states, "it begins with a single step." You have already taken your first step by beginning this book. You have believed enough to read this far. Let that be the first step. Now, keep reading, let that be the next.

Loneliness

Whenever we feel the need to reach out yet no one is there to reciprocate, loneliness ensues. Sometimes our loneliness is valid—we don't have access to the specific help that we desire. At other times loneliness is caused by our own choice not to reach out to others (unhealthy detachment).

Fortunately, loneliness is one of the emotions over which we have the most control. Thanks to the variety of support groups, the internet and our own personal circles, there is always someone that we can reach out to, if we gather the energy to do so.

In the case of loss, often our loneliness is a yearning for the person or thing that we have lost. While we can't replace the exact thing or person we have lost, we can work through Step Eight to understand the void. We can minimize the pain of our loneliness with healthy steps toward healing.

When do you experience your most intense loneliness?

_____

_____

_____

_____

Who do you know that you could seek support from in these lonely times? List them out below. I started the list for you.

Name or Resource	Contact Information
Grief Steps Online	www.griefsteps.com

Sadness and Depression

It is important to note that there is a difference between sadness and depression. While we grieve, we should expect to feel sadness. The intensity of this sadness will differ with the type of loss we are grieving. Shedding tears and being emotional often constitute sadness—not depression. If you find yourself immobilized, unable to concentrate, sleeping too much or too little, you are grieving, You will likely experience grief and sadness through the following traits (although these should be temporary):

- weakness and feeling drained
- loss of appetite
- extreme fatigue
- extreme irritability
- unresponsiveness
- inability to focus or concentrate
- feeling hopeless or powerless
- aches and pains
- lack of personal hygiene
- a feeling that the world is not a safe place

Depression is estimated to affect over 7 million Americans each year, with women being twice as likely to suffer as men. New York University's School of Medicine offers an online screening test that can be helpful for determining if you have depression. You can find the screening at http://www.med.nyu.edu/Psych/screens/depres.html

---

The essential thing to remember is that the pain of grief is never constant and does not last forever. Let the river of pain flow away from you, as you begin to recognize the currents of healing.

Understanding Emotional Triggers

It is not only important to understand the emotions we are feeling, but more importantly to understand how these emotions affect us. It can be helpful to keep a journal documenting your "emotional triggers."

Cognitive experts have determined that what we think about creates our feelings, our feelings create our moods and our moods fuel our actions. In its most basic sense the equation looks like this:

Thoughts = feelings,
which = moods, which = actions
therefore *Thoughts = actions*

When we work this equation in reverse, we can see where our actions stem from. First, take an action and ask yourself what type of mood you were in when you did it. Then ask yourself what feelings led to that mood. Lastly, ask yourself what thoughts you were feeling. This process may be tenuous at first, but the more often you do it, the easier it will become. This is an excellent way to get in touch with your thoughts and feelings, and to see how they affect your life, through actions and behavior.

Once you have done this exercise a few times, you will be able to recognize "triggers." When you recognize a thought process, you will know what mood and action it will lead to. Knowing this gives you the opportunity to change your thoughts and thus change the eventual action. This process is where the cliché, "Change your mind, change your life," stems from.

In the grid below, I completed a sample entry to show how this might work.

List an action	What mood were you in when you did the action	What thoughts were running through your mind when you did that action
Did not eat for two days.	Depressed and sad.	Thinking that without my loved one, life would never feel complete again.

Can you see how the "thoughts" would lead to the mood and the action? If the person would change their base thoughts, the mood and action would also change. This is the domino effect. Changing the thought pattern to, "I am lonely. I miss my loved one. These times are very difficult and there will always be a void—BUT I know that life has other wonderful moments in store for me." This subtle change in thought can yield big results in altering mood and action. Over the course of the next week, use the grid on the next page to log your own actions, moods and thoughts.

List an action	What mood were you in when you did the action	What thoughts were running through your mind when you did that action

Looking back on the grid on the proceeding page, what are some alternative thoughts you could use to reprogram actions that left you feeling sad, lonely or empty? Choose a few entries from the grid and record an alternate thought in the space provided below.

_____
_____
_____
_____
_____
_____
_____
_____
_____
_____
_____
_____
_____
_____
_____
_____
_____
_____
_____
_____
_____
_____
_____
_____
_____
_____
_____
_____

Notes:

Step Three:
Expressing Our Emotions
Through Active Grieving
and Acknowledgement

Purpose: To acknowledge the reality of our loss and engage in healthy, active grieving.

♦

"Trying to hide or escape our grief is often
more painful than experiencing grief."
~ **Brook Noel**

As we emerge from shock's grip, more and more emotions flood forward. It often feels like a roller-coaster as we dip back and forth between emotions. Remember how in Step One we created a space to honor our emotions? We do the same in Step Three—only now we will have many more emotions to face. Our shock has begun to subside, allowing us more resources with which to confront these confusing emotions. As painful as it may be, we must face them. Look again at the list of negative emotions in the preceding chapter. Do you want those emotions to lodge in your heart and impact your world? My guess is that you do not.

Notice that I don't use the word "acceptance" as part of this Step. Few of us are willing to "accept" our loss. How can we with the void it has left within us? The good news is that we don't have to accept our loss. We don't have to like it. We don't have to put on a "Pollyanna attitude" and march through our days as if we are "just fine."

What we are aiming for is acknowledgement. We need to acknowledge the reality of the loss in our lives and the void it has left behind. We don't get over our loss, but we can adapt to the life we have now.

How do we acknowledge our loss? We take the emotions that are within us and move them outside of us. We quit suppressing our pain and instead we purge it into the real world. We may complete this purging by:

· Journaling our emotions and sharing them with a trusted friend.

· Joining a support group and talking to others about our loss.

· Confiding in a close friend about how we feel.

· Seeking the help of a professional and vocalizing our loss to them.

· Learning to talk about our loss with others when the subject arises.

· Joining a trusted support site like GriefSteps® (www.griefsteps.com) and sharing our story with others.

What method is most appealing to you for acknowledging your loss? Choose from the above list or write down ideas of your own.

_____

_____

_____

_____

_____

_____

_____

_____

Why is it so important to share these feelings with others? When we do so we give them life, we acknowledge their reality. Think about it. We have so many thoughts that twirl in our heads. Many of our worries never happen. They are preoccupations or silly things we wouldn't vocalize. When we take a thought or feeling and express it in the real world, we give it credibility, we move it outside of ourselves and acknowledge its realness. Perhaps you can recall one of your own thinking patterns that seemed so "credible" when it existed solely in your mind. When you took this same thinking pattern (they are usually unhealthy patterns) and shared it with a trusted friend, he or she could poke many holes in it. Releasing our emotions externally, automatically gives them a "reality test." While this may not overtly create change, change is indeed occurring. We are no longer living and thinking on "autopilot," but instead with purpose. We are chipping away the barrier that grief can build within us when left untended and unmonitored. We are opening a pathway that can lead to wholeness.

Understanding our deepest questions is an important step to complete before entering into the actual exercises. Examine your loss with the questions below.

What specifically is the hardest part of your loss for you to face?

_____

_____

_____

_____

_____

From what reality are you trying to escape?

_____

_____

_____

_____

Know that when your grief journey takes you close to these answers you are likely to take a step back or recoil. Realize and respect what is hard for you. But then dig past it, or dig around it, so that you can move forward toward acknowledgement and release. Many people know this as "action therapy." By using action you move beyond the problem, thus dissolving the problem. You've literally "answered" and "solved" your problem through the use of positive and repetitive action.

Make A Space

If you're like me, you may find it helpful to schedule a "Vacation for Feeling." In order for me to truly get in touch with how I felt, I had to make a safe space for the feelings to surface. My day-to-day life as a CEO and Mom is hectic and crazy, and doesn't allow me a single sidestep. Only by taking several days away, with the sole intention of exposing my grief, was I then able to let my emotions rise to the surface. In the safety of a closed room, I could feel my sadness. There was no one there to see me as "weak," and no one there that I had to care for. My only "roommate" was my grief.

Where can you create a space for your grief? When can you schedule it?

_____

_____

_____

_____

_____

While it might seem day-to-day demands make "getting away" impossible—that is often a scenario created internally. When you explain this need to those who are close to you, I have often found they are very helpful in finding a solution to help you get the space you need. In essence—there isn't time NOT to get away—the damage you do internally from "trying to be strong" will ultimately hurt you and those around you.

Who do you need to talk to in order to create this space?

_____

_____

_____

_____

How will this space help you?

_____

_____

_____

_____

_____

Journaling to Music

Writing about feelings has proven a successful venue for many people. When you write, don't worry about punctuation, grammar or how your writing might sound to another person. When you are writing, just aim to express your innermost thoughts. Write whatever comes to mind. Dig for words. Anything goes when journaling. You can keep your journal or burn your pages—whatever is most comfortable for you. I recommend keeping your journal as a chronicle of your journey. However, if several pages are extremely sensitive, you may choose to burn those pages or keep them in a password protected file on a computer; or if handwritten, under lock and key. You want your journal to be a private and secure place where you can explore your feelings without concern.

The actual physical act of "writing" can be very rewarding. It shows a respect and caring for ourselves, since we take the time to create a thoughtful page that can be held and reread. We are valuing our abstract thoughts by giving them a "physical existence." I have worked with many people who have found this process both cleansing and healing (even those people who swore they would never enjoy writing). Being able to look back on a collection of writing can be very encouraging—as we see how far we have come.

If you have a difficult time starting to write, try listening to some emotional or moving music. Let the notes evoke your feelings and write about what you feel. Take a moment to scan through a nearby radio until you find a melody or music that elicits some feeling within you (can be positive or negative). Use the space below to write about anything that comes to mind while listening to your chosen music.

Journaling: Sentence-Starters

Using a sentence-starter can also be helpful. Try writing "I feel…" and then completing the sentence. Continue doing that over and over. The more times you do this, the more the sentence-starter will reveal. Or you can use a sentence-starter that names an emotion, "I feel angry because…"

Complete the sentences below to get an idea of how this works. Don't over-analyze what you are going to write; simply read the question and let the words flow in spontaneous response.

I am sad because…

_____

_____

I am angry because…

_____

_____

I feel anxious about…

_____

_____

I am depressed about…

_____

_____

I feel lonely when…

_____

_____

I am scared that…

_____

_____

The hardest part is…

_____

_____

I miss…

_____

_____

I regret that…

_____

_____

I can't handle…

_____

_____

I wish I…

_____

_____

If only I could…

_____

_____

I never should have…

_____

_____

I am disappointed because…

_____

_____

Sometimes I…

_____

_____

Expanding on Your Sentence-Starters

You'll know when you hit a sentence-starter that you need to work with further because the words will flow out quickly and easily and will not fit in the space above. Use a separate journal or the blank pages at the back of this book to continue writing. Don't stop.

Poetry

Poetry creates a bridge (of feelings) between the material world and the world of creativity and spirit. Visiting and/or joining a poetry group can have an extraordinary effect on the way we heal our grief. Poets, by definition, get to the raw feelings behind the masks we all wear. When we are wearing the mask of grief, we may feel that others cannot possibly know the pain we are experiencing, yet we must still continue living day to day in spite of our tremendous loss. As a result, we may feel out of touch with friends who have not experienced such a loss. We may feel that our level of feeling is unacceptable to others. Feelings are the dynamic force behind poetry groups. Within these groups you will find a welcome and sensitive home for the powerful expression of your grief through using written and spoken word.

Check your local paper for poetry readings or "open mic" nights. Many bookstores and colleges conduct such events. Attend the readings and ask participants about other local events or groups in your area.

You can also write poetry on your own, or write it on your own and share through online poetry groups. Many books exist that can fuel creativity and offer guidance. Check the writing/reference section at your local bookstore. If you would like to purchase a book on poetry, I strongly recommend *POEM CRAZY: Freeing Your Life with Word* by Susan G. Wooldridge (ISBN 0609800981). Another good book is *WRITING THE NATURAL WAY: Using Right-Brain Techniques to Release Your Expressive Powers* by George Rico, PhD and Tyler Volk (ISBN 0874779618).

It can be extremely cleansing to spend a morning, once a week, at a cafe or a park, writing poetry in a beautiful journal. Don't worry about form—just creatively put down words to express yourself. The exercises on the following pages can help you get started.

Utilize Freewriting

Before reading further, take a moment to write down how you are feeling at this very moment in the space provided below.

_____

_____

_____

_____

_____

Freewriting is the process of recording thoughts and feelings on the fly. Instead of analyzing what you are writing, or worrying about form or structure, you just write continually. There are only two rules for freewriting—you can't stop moving your pen or pencil—and you can't erase anything you have written. The point of this exercise is to dig past the surface and into your soul—and then to give your soul a space to express itself. Freewriting works especially well for those who are intimidated by the thought of journaling and it can also be used in conjunction with journaling. I recommend a 5-minute freewrite first thing in the morning. When we first wake, we can access our innermost thoughts more readily. If you are leery about trying a freewrite, that is all the more reason to push yourself to do so. You might find that this can help you uncover much of your inner life. Try to make a commitment to freewrite at least four mornings each week for five minutes. Set a timer for yourself. When the timer dings, stop writing.

Put down this book and try a five minute freewrite. Avoid excuses and just take action. Use the space below and on the following pages to write. If you follow the rules and don't stop writing, you should be able to fill the entire space (or most of it) in the five minute allotment.

_____

_____

_____

_____

_____

_____

_____

_____

_____

_____

_____

_____

_____

_____

_____

_____

_____

_____

_____

_____

_____

_____

_____

_____

_____

_____

_____

_____

_____

_____

_____

_____

_____

_____

_____

_____

_____

_____

_____

_____

Now, take a moment to write down how you feel right now. What did freewriting show you?

_____

_____

_____

_____

Living for Today

Many times after we experience loss we wish we would have had more time to experience life as we once knew it. Loss is inevitable. We will experience many more losses in our lives and lose things we currently hold precious. Those who move through grief work naturally come to share one predominant trait—they live in the moment. Their list of regrets becomes short, because they make the most of each day. Many times, after experiencing loss, we learn, perhaps for the first time, how precious "a moment" can be. We learn how temporary and fluid our world is. Living for today can help you honor your grief by finding something "good" in the rubble. It can also help you have less regrets and guilt should you experience more loss in your future. We need to learn to live in our today—if we spend our moments worried about tomorrow, or trying to change the past, our "today's" become empty "yesterdays."

Use the space below to write about how you can live more in the moment. Also take a moment to appreciate all the current blessings in your life—both great and small.

_____

_____

_____

_____

_____

_____

_____

_____

_____

_____

_____

_____

_____

_____

_____

_____

_____

_____

_____

_____

_____

_____

The Serenity Prayer

It's amazing how we will fight for control—even to our own detriment. Relinquishing the illusion of control can be frightening. So much of life's unhappiness stems from trying to exert power over things we are powerless to control. When we learn to quit focusing our energies on the unchangeable, and instead focus on where we can be effective, we take a large step on the pathway to peace. The Serenity Prayer so beautifully summarizes this point,

> God grant me the Serenity
> to accept the things I cannot change;
> Courage to change the things I can;
> and Wisdom to know the difference.
> **~Reinhold Neibuhr**

This prayer is one we would all do well to practice daily. When we truly understand what we cannot change, and face the things we can with courage, we relieve stress, unease and unhappiness. Read the Serenity Prayer several times, slowly then answer the questions below.

What have you been trying to control that is truly out of your control?

_____

_____

_____

_____

_____

How does it feel to contemplate letting these things go and accepting that you cannot change them?

_____

_____

_____

_____

_____

Write about the things you can control with change.

_____

_____

_____

_____

_____

How can you face them with courage?

_____

_____

_____

_____

_____

What situations confuse you? Why are you unsure if you can exert control or not? Write about them.

_____

_____

_____

_____

_____

Who do you know that could help you develop the wisdom you need to make decisions about the things that confuse you?

_____

_____

_____

_____

In the Appendix you'll find this prayer printed on a pocket reminder card along with other cards that carry valuable messages for your journey. Cut these cards out and keep the ones that resonate with you close by or within reach.

Realize Your Resilience

When we face loss, it can be of help to remember other times in our past when we have faced loss, and have come out okay. Even if the events were small or seemingly insignificant, they were still training and conditioning, that evidence the resilience of the human spirit. In a sense, we experience many "mini-deaths" throughout our lifetime, or as Judith Viorst calls them, "necessary losses." We separate from our parents; we lose our freedom to play, in turn for work and accountability. We lose our childhood, baby teeth, myths (such as Santa Claus), wisdom teeth. As we age we lose our youth, health, dexterity, mental awareness, eye sight. We lose weight when we diet. We lose our parents, grand parents, pets, friends. We might lose our homes, our jobs, our children to college and marriage. Loss is a natural conclusion to so many of our life experiences. Every beginning must, at some point, have an end.

In the space below, write about a loss you have experienced in the past. Note how you felt at the time.

_____

_____

_____

Now write about the process of overcoming that loss.

_____

_____

_____

How do you feel now, when looking back at this loss? Can you see the strength or resilience you found?

_____

_____

_____

Personally, I find this a great way to gather strength. There have been times in my life when I truly thought I was experiencing life's worst pain. I can remember in the moment thinking... "If I can get through this, I can get through anything." I remember how hopeless life felt—yet I pushed forward. And now my life is so rich—a richness I never would have uncovered had I not forged forward. That's not to say there won't be problems. Life will always be filled with unexpected turmoil. However, I have gathered a new strength for facing this turmoil.

Positives and Negatives

Sometimes taking a basic look at the pros and cons of facing our grief can help us gather the motivation to move forward. Explore the negative aspects behind not handling your grief. For example, when we suppress our grief and choose not to face it, we may be angry, easily irritable, impatient, sad, missing moments of joy, and even facing depletion of faith. Use the chart below to list your own pros and cons.

Pros for Facing My Grief	Cons for Facing My Grief

Multiple Grief

Some people have multiple situations they are dealing with on top of their grief. Perhaps an elderly parent is ill, you are sending a child off to college, you are going through menopause, or a career change, or completing college or some other challenging life situation. These multiple situations can halt, delay or complicate the primary grieving process. When we have many stressful experiences, much of our emotional energy is funneled into these stressors. We are left with little reserve. Yet, in order to heal we must find a way to cope with each stressor, while still feeling and exploring our grief.

Although one experience may stand out in your mind, any other times of loss are likely to be important as well. Even things that might seem small or insignificant in the face of tragedy can complicate the grieving process when they accumulate. Soon we find ourselves stuck in a web of turmoil, unable to unravel our complicated feelings. Many events have mixed together and we can't pull on a single string to undue the knot—instead a tug on a single string just makes the knot tighter.

To work through Multiple Grief, it's important to recognize each of the components that you are grieving. Once you have identified those components you can begin to focus on healing. Take your time in identifying these components—they may not come to the surface at first! If you find that you are still facing acute grief after a long period, you may want to come back to this exercise. Sometimes we suppress other losses that get caught up in the web. For example, a loss you are facing now might remind you of the abense of a parent during a difficult period in your life. To find the wholeness we hunger for, we must grieve each of our losses completely. Explore the impact of multiple grief in your life by answering the following questions.

(Exercise adapted from I Wasn't Ready to Say Goodbye: surviving, coping and healing after the sudden death of a loved one by Brook Noel and Pamela D. Blair, Ph.D. ISBN 1-891400-27-4, Published by Champion Press, Ltd.)

What is the most recent experience you are grieving?

_____

_____

_____

_____

_____

_____

Are there any other experiences in the past 5 years that you grieved, or are grieving for?

_____

_____

_____

_____

_____

_____

_____

_____

_____

_____

_____

_____

_____

_____

_____

_____

_____

For each of the experiences you listed, did you move through the different stages of grieving, or did you stop somewhere in the process without ever fully coming to terms with your grief? If you stopped, mid-process, where did you stop?

_____

_____

_____

_____

_____

_____

_____

_____

_____

_____

_____

_____

_____

_____

_____

_____

Are there any other times of loss that your current experience resurrects in your mind?

_____

_____

_____

_____

_____

_____

_____

_____

_____

_____

_____

_____

_____

_____

_____

_____

_____

_____

_____

When you have listed all of your grief you will know it because you will feel both a sadness and a relief inside. Until that point, you will feel a gnawing ache, as if you are trying to excavate a very embedded rock. You do not need to remember, recall or record everything at once. Do not force it. Simply continue returning to this exercise, excavating a bit more each time. Remember we are taking step after step on our journey.

Hurtful Self-Talk

Hurtful self-talk can block the grieving process—keeping you stuck. Sometimes it's easier to play "negative tapes" in our mind than to move through our pain toward healing. The healing process is tough—but there is a light at the end. Overcoming hurtful self-talk is an important step toward that light. The following statements are examples of commonly-felt hurtful self-talk that may run through our minds. Don't be ashamed if you identify with these statements. Place a check by each statement that you identify with, as a way to acknowledge it. Next, we will look at how to overcome these thoughts.

- My loved one is with God for a reason, so I shouldn't feel bad
- Grief is a mental illness
- It is wrong to feel anger at the deceased and it shouldn't be expressed
- If I acknowledge the loss, I'm afraid I will die too
- I should have died first
- If I allow my grief to surface, I'll go crazy
- If I grieve, people will think I'm weak
- If I appear sad too often, it will bring my family down
- If I cry in church, my fellow congregants will think I've lost faith
- If my children see me grieving, it will make them feel worse
- The deceased wouldn't want me to grieve
- Our life together was always happy—I don't want to remember the bad times
- I should have _____ (fill in the blank!)
- I should grin and bear it and put it behind me
- If I stop grieving people will expect me to be happy again.

When you find yourself running on the treadmill of hurtful self-talk it is important to come up with a positive statement for balance. Write down your destructive or hurtful thought and then write down a more positive, realistic thought. For example, "The deceased wouldn't want me to grieve," is hurtful. You could write, "The deceased would understand and respect the full spectrum of my emotions." Whenever a negative thought enters your mind, replace it with a positive, more realistic statement. Try "reprogramming" your hurtful self-talk on the following page. Continue to add statements along with their positive counterparts as they occur to you throughout your journey.

Reprogramming Self-Talk

Hurtful Statement:

_____

_____

_____

Positive Statement:

_____

_____

_____

Hurtful Statement:

_____

_____

_____

Positive Statement:

_____

_____

_____

Hurtful Statement:

_____

_____

_____

Positive Statement:

_____

_____

_____

Hurtful Statement:

_____

_____

_____

Positive Statement:

_____

_____

_____

Can We Grieve Too Much?

While it is important to face our grief and move through it, there is a danger in grieving "too much." Some people get stuck in their grief, and wrap themselves in the process without the goal of moving forward. The process of grief becomes comforting, a way to link themselves to their loss.

Some people find themselves longing for any link to their loved one, even if it is painful. It is not uncommon for bereaved persons to fear they will forget their loved one's smile, or how they looked, or sounded, or walked. Instead of working through the process of letting go, they hold onto everything they can, scared to let the slightest memory slip away.

Dr. Forest Church, author of *LIFELINES: Holding on (and Letting Go)* points out that, "Once the death of another person [or our loss] becomes an excuse for not going on with one's own life, or not being able to live fully and abundantly, then that's pathological."

When we use our loss as an excuse to hide in our past, we are entering a pathological state which demonstrates the need to go back and make sure we have completed each of the Grief Steps®.

Are there any ways that you are using your loss to hide in your past? Be honest and open in the space provided below.

_____

_____

_____

_____

_____

_____

_____

_____

_____

_____

_____

_____

_____

_____

_____

_____

_____

_____

_____

_____

Step Four:
Understanding Your Story

Purpose: To find a beginning, middle and end so that we may cease obsessive thinking and move beyond the story of our loss toward healing.

◆

"Essential grief is a tearing down and then building back up..."
~ **Ashley Davis Prend, TRANSCENDING LOSS**

In her book *Writing to Heal the Soul*, author Susan Zimmerman says, "It is a story that has torn your heart into pieces, and it is a story of beauty, because your heart couldn't have been torn without your having first loved and somehow lost something that you loved. Now is the time to begin honoring your story. A friend sent me a note that said simply, 'Blessed are the cracked, for they shall let the light in.'"

The need to 'solve the story' explains why it is so natural (and so necessary) to talk with others about our loss. Over and over again, grievers tell their stories, attempting to make sense of them, attempting to understand the cycle.

Often, there are many ways to collect information. When we have enough clues we can piece together a story that will allow our questioning to lessen. As our questions lessen, we create more room to heal. If we find ourselves reluctant to complete the exercises to understand our story, that is a signal that we are fighting the reality of our loss. Chances are more work is needed with the first three Grief Steps®.

Dr. Ann Kaiser Stearns, author of *Coming Back: Rebuilding Lives After Crisis and Loss* offers the following suggestions: "Make a conscious effort to identify what is not making sense to you about your loss or crisis. You might ask yourself: What is it about the situation... that is most puzzling or troubling to me? What part of grief is troubling me? What other things are troubling me?"

You have a story that only you can tell. You have lessons that you have learned, feelings that you have felt, moments that have moved you.

Before beginning the journey to understand your story, ask yourself the three questions Dr. Stearns suggests:

1. What is it about the situation that is most puzzling or troubling to me?

_____

_____

_____

_____

_____

2. What part of grief is troubling me?

_____

_____

_____

_____

_____

3. What other things are troubling me?

_____

_____

_____

_____

_____

_____

_____

The need to find a beginning, middle and end applies to all types of losses. Talking to others will help you get the information you need to find your own beginning, middle and end. This information-gathering can be a major catalyst in moving past the grief of "what happened?" to the process of rebuilding. It allows the mind to cycle through the event in its entirety, instead of stopping to question and getting lost in the who, what, when, where, why and how.

Uncovering the components of your story can be done with the aid of the worksheet on the following page. You will see that there are three columns labeled: BEGINNING, MIDDLE and END. Write what you know for certain about each of these areas. Then write down the questions you have.

Worksheet for Uncovering Your Story

Beginning	Middle	End
What I know for certain:	What I know for certain:	What I know for certain:
Questions I have:	Questions I have:	Questions I have:

You have taken the first steps toward uncovering your story, now it is time to dig a little deeper. On the worksheet below, list the questions you have in the first column. In the second column, write down who could help you uncover the answer—also list a goal date for contacting that person or resource. In column three, write your findings after you have completed the task in column two.

The question I have is....	The person or resource that could help me with an answer is...	The person or resource revealed that...

Moving forward requires that you define a beginning, middle and end for your experience. Once you have accomplished this you can move on with a new perspective, feeling confident that you have acknowledged, and come to the most thorough understanding possible at this time. When you have gathered the answers needed for your beginning, middle and end, block out several hours of quiet time to write your story in its entirety. Because a complete version of your story could well be a small book in and of itself, I have decided not to include blank space in this workbook. Instead, I recommend you buy a special journal just for that purpose and work with your story over a period of time.

Step Five: Finding Forgiveness

Purpose: To release ourselves from unnecessary pain through the act of forgiveness.

♦

"The important thing to remember when it comes to forgiving is that forgiveness doesn't make the other person right; it *makes you free.*"
~ **Stormie Omartian,**
PRAYING GOD'S WILL FOR YOUR LIFE

Forgiveness is one of the hardest Steps of the grieving process and one where many people, who are otherwise doing fine in their grief journey, get stuck. I know firsthand how difficult forgiveness can be since it was one of my hardest lessons in grief.

When our anger gets stuck, it doesn't let us forgive. That is why this Step comes so much later in the grieving process. We have to release our anger and our pent-up emotions before we can get to the place where forgiveness is possible.

How do we know if we need to forgive? We know because we feel a gnawing sadness inside of us, although we may not know the cause. We do the releasing exercises, but an ache still lingers. Nine times out of ten, if we have completed the other emotional exercises of grief, this ache is caused by our inability to (or choice not to) forgive.

The interesting thing about unforgiveness is that it is a lot like guilt. It is a useless emotion that mostly hurts the person who feels it. Your inability to forgive anything or any person in your world may hurt someone else a bit, but I guarantee it hurts you and your world a hundred times more.

Forgiveness Brings Freedom

With forgiveness, we face our emotions, the good and the bad. Instead of glossing over how things actually happened, we face the reality of how our cards were dealt and how we feel the hurt and anger within. When we are unforgiving, we see our own dark sides. Only through facing this darkness, can we release ourselves from its toll. An unforgiving nature is very costly in our lives. We may find ourselves attaching to other people in unhealthy ways, punishing other people or losing hope in the world and in our peers. As you can see, we are the ones that suffer most when our hearts and minds won't let us forgive.

The first step in forgiveness is to understand all the elements of the incident we are trying to forgive. Instead of letting it hang above us like a black cloud, we say exactly how we feel, openly and honestly, admitting our pain.

Who and what are we forgiving exactly? We are forgiving anything and everything that needs to be forgiven. We may be forgiving God, a person who harmed us or a person who harmed someone we love. We may be forgiving our parents, our society, our world, or ourselves. Forgiveness does not mean that we are condoning hurtful actions. It doesn't mean that we accept the sometimes evil and inhumane actions of others. Forgiveness does not mean that we forget how much we hurt. Forgiveness simply means that we acknowledge the deep pain we feel, but choose to move past that pain. We forgive those who contributed to our pain and let their actions become part of our past. We can dislike what someone has done to us, but we can still forgive them and allow them to be someone new, instead of freeze-framing them in that hurtful place, that hurts us too.

Make a list of the people or situations that you are having a hard time forgiving.

_____

_____

_____

_____

_____

_____

_____

_____

Sometimes looking at this in a different perspective can be extremely helpful. Think back and recall a time when you did something hurtful to someone. Perhaps you said something "off the cuff" that hurt someone's feelings, or perhaps you did something you were ashamed of. Take a few moments to recollect the most vivid example that you can and record it below.

_____

_____

_____

_____

_____

_____

_____

_____

Now think through the series of events that led up to your action. You did something hurtful and how did the other person respond? Did they eventually forgive you? What would happen if they hadn't? What would happen if the person had stayed angry at you for that action? You made a mistake, a bad decision, or didn't think before acting, and if they didn't forgive you, they would never be able to see you how you are now. Unforgiveness chains people to their painful actions. We freeze that painful time. Can you see how that person would be missing all you could offer? Or how that person could become so focused on the pain you caused, that they would miss the other good happening around them?

Write about how the situation on the previous page played out.

_____

_____

_____

_____

_____

_____

_____

_____

Forgiving people also serves as a huge release. When we don't forgive, we become in a sense, that person's "judge and jury." Our unforgiveness is "their sentence." However, it is not our job to be the judge and jury over anyone. It is our job to live life. Besides, the responsibility of "judge" is one that is stressful and pain-ridden. It is certainly not a role any of us need to assume ever—especially during grief.

As I rediscovered the role of faith in my own life, I found comfort in the New Testament when it came to topics of forgiveness and judgment. I was able to see that Jesus, when faced with judgment did not react harmfully, but blessed others. This act of non-judgment allowed Jesus to retain a peaceful heart. Had he chosen to judge, he would have wrapped himself in angst. Slowly, through my studying and reading, I came to accept that it was not my job to judge anyone (nor my right). Likewise, it is not my job to defend myself to anyone who tries to judge me.

At one point in my life, I was so concerned with how others saw me. I wanted to make sure everyone had the actual facts on which to base their thoughts and opinions. If someone held what I perceived to be an unfair view, I would go to great lengths to get my own "evidence" into their hands or to defend myself. I cannot tell you how exhausting this was. Liberation came when I made the decision to truly "let go." I began to focus only on blessing others—no matter what they thought of me. I quit trying to "present my case" and instead began to live my life. Everyday I set out to live the best life, and do the best work, I am capable of doing. I will let that action speak for itself.

Who are you trying to play judge and jury for?

_____
_____
_____
_____
_____
_____
_____
_____
_____
_____
_____
_____
_____

How would releasing that role make you feel?

_____
_____
_____
_____
_____
_____
_____
_____
_____
_____
_____
_____
_____

Letter Writing

Focus on a situation or experience you feel angry about or that you have been unable to forgive. Write a letter to the person or situation your emotions are directed toward. Write down everything that you are mad, sad or upset about. Let it all out—don't hold back. Use any words you can to describe your feelings and emotions. If you don't like to write, speak your mind into a tape recorder, holding nothing back. Feel the release that occurs inside you as you do this. Expect tears. Expect all the anger and ugliness to emerge as you purge the incident from your system. When you are done, take the letter and burn it, or the tape and crush it. Let this serve as a symbol of your forgiveness. If you become stuck in the pain again, repeat this exercise.

Letter writing can also be used to "keep in touch" with a loved one and to "keep in touch" with ourselves. Many people find a sense of release when putting pen to paper. Use the space below to write a short letter to someone who is on your mind.

_____

_____

_____

_____

_____

_____

_____

_____

_____

_____

_____

_____

_____

_____

_____

_____

_____

_____

_____

_____

_____

_____

_____

_____

Self-Forgiveness and Self-Love

Even when we have been able to forgive those who have hurt us, we often cannot forgive ourselves. Many of us unfairly hold ourselves prisoner to unrealistic standards that we would never expect of another person.

Self-Forgiveness Reality Check Exercise: Recall an incident for which you have not forgiven yourself. Write about the incident in the space below.

_____

_____

_____

_____

_____

_____

Now close your eyes. Imagine a morning where you are sitting in your kitchen with a cup of coffee, a morning when a dear friend knocks on your door. Your friend is trying to hold back her tears, but you know she has been crying from her tear-stained face. You invite her in and she crumbles into the chair across from you. When you ask what is wrong, she bursts into tears, mumbling her story of sadness through strained breath. Imagine that her story of sadness is the same or parallel to the event recorded in your journal.

Visualize yourself advising your friend. What do you say? Do you make her feel worse, by amplifying her mistake? Do you lecture her, implying she should hold herself hostage to her mistake and let it cause unhappiness throughout her life? Or do you take a different tactic? Take a moment to thoroughly visualize your response, then write about it below.

_____

_____

_____

_____

_____

_____

_____

_____

_____

_____

_____

A true friend would not let another friend suffer indefinitely—even for the worst of actions. Instead, a true friend would suggest accountability while encouraging self-forgiveness and forward movement. Try offering yourself that same wisdom. Use the space below to write an affirming letter to yourself—one that promotes self-forgiveness and forward movement.

_____
_____
_____
_____
_____
_____
_____
_____
_____
_____
_____
_____
_____
_____
_____
_____
_____
_____
_____
_____
_____
_____
_____
_____
_____
_____
_____

Self-love and self-forgiveness come when we treat ourselves
as we would a dear friend.

Unblocking Unforgiveness

If we have lived a life where we have not practiced forgiveness, we have likely built a wall of pain and hurt inside. Unearthing all of this unforgiveness will be a major step toward healing.

In the space below (use additional pages if necessary) write down everything you can recall from your life that has gone unforgiven. Include the ways you have not forgiven others and include times when you did not forgive yourself. Let this list build throughout the upcoming month.

_____

_____

_____

_____

_____

_____

_____

_____

_____

_____

_____

_____

_____

_____

_____

_____

_____

_____

_____

_____

_____

_____

_____

This list serves as your pathway to freedom. It will take time, but working through each event on your list, by using the exercises in this chapter, will grant you peace and freedom from the bondages brought-on by not forgiving one another or yourself.

Simple Self-Love Exercise

For those of us who have not practiced self-love, it can be a difficult concept to grasp. Begin with a simple gesture of self-directed love. Perhaps it is five minutes of uninterrupted reading, or a hot bubble bath, or a walk in nature, or meeting a friend for a cup of coffee. It can be anything that validates the importance of treating yourself well. Create a list in the space below of simple ways you can express self-love. Affirm your value daily by practicing one of these exercises.

Notes:

Step Six: Finding Faith

Purpose: To explore, rebuild and repair our faith.

◆

"Whatever religion we choose to accept, we have to recognize that it has led others through their 'dark valley of the shadow of death' in the past, and it will do so again. We are not the first to tread that bleak path, even as we know we will not be the last."
~ **Robert J. Marx, Susan Wengerhoff Davidson,**
FACING THE ULTIMATE LOSS

There is a reason that faith comes later in the grieving journey rather than earlier. Faith is a complex and difficult concept to grapple with on any given day, let alone during a time when it has been pushed to the edge. As Robert J. Marx and Susan Wengerhoff Davidson write in *Facing the Ultimate Loss: coping with the death of a child*, "All we know is that we are in pain, and quick fixes are the things we reject most quickly. In a time of suffering, we all recognize that faith is not an easy thing to grasp. There are so many moments when we are too depressed to even listen to what our faith has to offer."

It is for this very reason that faith comes later in our journey. We begin to seek out or reunite with our faith after we have faced many of the emotions of grief. That does not mean that God isn't with us while we grieve. Many people can, and do, find solace in the grace of God throughout their journey. But for many others, not only do we experience loss, but we may question the foundation of our spirituality. Suddenly we are living in a foggy world with a new question at every turn—questions that do not have easy answers. **Prior to completing the questions and exercises within this chapter, please read the Finding Faith chapter in the Grief Steps book (pages 139-153).**

Where is your focus? Some grievers focus on the tragedy itself, letting all the surrounding activities and gestures swirl into the oblivion of their grief. These grievers do not see, or quickly forget, the people that reached out to them, the people that sat with them late into the night to offer comfort. When we cannot see that "God is in the little things," that God is in people's gestures, we tend to stumble on our own faith.

Where and what have you been focusing on?

_____

_____

_____

_____

_____

_____

What little acts of kindness and caring could you also focus on?

_____

_____

_____

_____

_____

_____

_____

The Push-Pull of Comfort: Another reason people are conflicted by faith has to do with finding their own sense of peace. For many, the very thought of finding any solace or comfort seems a betrayal to their loss. "Why should I be happy when ____ will never know another day on earth?" "Who am I to seek comfort when I have lost my job and cannot amply provide for my family?" One hand reaches for the comfort that can only be provided by faith while the other hand pushes it away.

When we find ourselves engaged in the push-pull of faith, we must continue to work with the exercises that help us to seek meaning, redefine our life, and find purpose in our loss, to carry forward. When we commit to moving through this haze, our conflicting emotions become only temporary and we will be able to surpass them.

Do you see signs of the push-pull of comfort in your life? If so, record them here.

_____

_____

_____

_____

_____

Faith Communities and Anger

It's common to question God in these dark times. We may lose our faith in God, a faith we thought would never change or waiver. This is okay. The Psalms are filled with passages where God is questioned.

"My God, my God, why have you deserted me?
... Why are you so far away?
Won't you listen to my groans and come to my rescue?
... I cry out day and night, but you don't answer,
... and I can never rest."
~Psalm 22: 1,2 (Contemporary English Version)

We have the right to feel passing anger, but it is also important to not let our anger destroy our faith. In *The Grief Recovery Handbook*, John W. James and Russell Freidman write, "We have to be allowed to tell someone that we're angry at God and not be judged for it, or told that we're bad because of it. If not, this anger may persist forever and block spiritual growth. We've known people who never returned to their religion because they weren't allowed to express their true feelings. If this happens, the griever is cut off from one of the most powerful sources of support he or she might have." For most of us, this loss of faith is temporary and if we ask our clergy person or faith community, they will willingly help us with this struggle. It is common for grievers to yell, scream at God or lose faith. One should not feel guilty for such emotions. Like many other aspects of grief, this internal search is part of the process.

Are you angry at God? Write about your feelings honestly and openly in the space below.

_____
_____
_____
_____
_____
_____
_____

How does this anger make you feel?

_____
_____
_____
_____
_____

Are you in a faith community that can give you the support you need?

_____

_____

_____

_____

_____

_____

_____

If not, is there another support community available to you?

_____

_____

_____

_____

_____

_____

_____

If you find yourself in a faith community that cannot handle your anger, you must re-evaluate your needs. Your primary need is to be in a group of believers that can accept your human feelings. Seek out a support group or community that can walk with you through this dark time. If your faith is important to you, do not shut yourself off from it for fear that no one will understand or accept you. After you have moved through your journey, you may want to consider going back to the faith community where you could not find initial support and begin a support group.

Anger as Evidence of Faith

In its basic sense, our anger is an affirmation of our faith. Authors Marx and Davidson summarize this well when they write, "When we lose a child [or someone or something], we so often become the victims of our anger—anger at a husband or wife, anger at a doctor, even occasionally at the child who has been taken from us. Of all the rage we experience, none may be more bitter than our anger toward God. 'How could a loving and kind God do this to me?' Even the rage of a betrayed husband or wife could not be more bitter. After a lifetime of trust, how could that God of justice and loving-kindness allow this terrible injustice? The angry question can be seen as an affirmation and accusation. After all, the very anger we feel is based upon the fact that we believe. We cannot be angry with someone who does not exist."

Think about any anger you feel. How does that serve as a testament to your faith? Write about this discovery in the space below.

_____

_____

_____

_____

_____

_____

_____

_____

_____

_____

_____

_____

_____

_____

_____

_____

_____

_____

_____

_____

_____

What Do I Believe?

As we stand at our own crossroad, we must look at our life and evaluate our faith. Is our faith a part of us or is it simply something we have inherited and accepted blindly? Have we really believed prior to our loss—or have we just gone through the motions? What does faith mean to us? What do we seek to find? Once we identify our basic need and belief system, we can begin to move toward the communities and materials that will be the most helpful. Faith, by definition, should be something that encourages and supports us in our day-to-day living.

How did you come to your current faith?

_____

_____

_____

_____

_____

_____

_____

_____

_____

_____

_____

_____

_____

Is your current faith supporting your needs?

_____

_____

_____

_____

_____

_____

_____

_____

_____

_____

_____

_____

_____

The Act of Prayer

Praying does not require anything accept your own willingness. In a time of suffering do not be concerned about a "right" way to pray or a "wrong" way to pray. Take a walk and talk to God. Let Him know how you feel. Let Him know what you need. Think about this communication as you would any other relationship. If you were angry with someone, what would happen if you retreated into yourself instead of ever voicing your feelings? A wall would form between the two of you. When we communicate our innermost thoughts to God, as in any other relationship, we keep the walls at bay.

If you have built a wall between yourself and God, then begin to pray that the wall will crumble. Ask God how to reach and how to break the wall down. Remember that God is not forceful, He comes by invitation—He comes the moment you open your heart and ask Him to be present.

This process becomes especially important for anyone who is angry with God. While people may argue that our anger is misdirected, we need to forgive God in our hearts so that we may mend and move forward in our relationship with Him.

Write a note to God in the space provided below. Even if you are angry, welcome Him into your life. Let Him show you the way to forgiveness.

Notes:

Step Seven: Finding Meaning

Purpose: To understand that even the deepest tragedy can bring meaning, and to uncover that meaning.

> "To everything there is a season,
> and a time for every purpose under Heaven:
> A time to be born, and a time to die;
> A time to break down and a time to build up;
> A time to weep, and a time to laugh;
> A time to mourn, and a time to dance."
> **~Ecclesiastes 3:1-4**

When we grapple with our losses, we are forced to reconsider some assumptions about our selves and our lives. We may feel vulnerable and that life is tenuous. We may begin to question whether or not the world is meaningful and orderly. We may see ourselves as weak and needy.

You may have thought, "[Enter your loss] can't happen to me." But it did happen and you may no longer feel the world is a safe place. Feelings of vulnerability can bring on a sense of doom.

In *Trust After Trauma*, Dr. Aphrodite Matsakis writes, "The just world philosophy cannot explain what happened to you. You used to think that if you were careful, honest, and good, you could avoid disaster. But the trauma taught you that all of your best efforts could not prevent the worst from happening. So, while you would like to believe that the world is orderly, and that good is rewarded and evil is punished, you had an experience that contradicts these beliefs."

Explore how your experience has changed your perception of the world around you in the space below and on the following page.

_____

_____

_____

_____

_____

Exploring Tough Questions about Meaning

It is best to answer these questions when you have uninterrupted time. Also make sure you have cycled through many of the difficult emotions that accompany loss. Attempting to "rush" these answers will only lead to frustration. These are also wonderful questions to explore within a support group.

Before beginning your journey to uncover meaning, there are some important points I want to cover. First, finding meaning does not happen overnight. You don't suddenly wake up one morning with some secure sense of "this all makes sense now!" Usually, meaning comes with time and reflection.

When my brother died a senseless death, I hardly believed there could ever be any meaning. Yet now, six years later, I have found myself in a place I would never have been without this experience. I have created books, web sites and tools that have walked countless grievers through their dark journey. I have received countless letters and e-mails, expressing gratitude for the support I have been able to offer.

When 9/11 occurred and people scrambled for support material, I had one of the only books in existence that dealt specifically with sudden death. However, all of this doesn't make Caleb's death any more "right" or "just." I still don't have to "like" it. But I can begin to understand that perhaps there is a meaning to everything, a structure, a form—even if it is a structure that I don't like.

> *Finding meaning and understanding our losses does not happen overnight. It takes commitment and time to heal.*

After reading the above paragraphs, sit for a moment and think about your own grief experience. What initial thoughts and reactions do you have to the concept of "finding meaning"?

_____

_____

_____

_____

_____

_____

_____

_____

_____

_____

_____

_____

In Step Four of the *Grief Steps®* book, I spoke of a businessman named Logan, who had been unexpectedly let go from his high-profile job at the age of forty-eight. After devoting his life to the betterment of a company, the company let him go in a down-sizing. After Logan worked through his initial shock and anger, he began to work through the steps of redefinition and finding meaning. Logan ended up totally changing his life. He downsized his home life by putting his dream house up for sale. He bought a much smaller home, paid off as much debt as possible, and began a small cafe and bookstore with his wife. The two had grown apart over the years, yet the pursuit of this new dream brought them close in ways they never had imagined. Yet Logan could have chosen many different routes. He could have skipped these steps and chosen to wrap himself in anger and bitterness. Instead, he looked at what he knew for sure. He knew he loved to read and loved books. He knew he had always wanted his own business. He knew his relationship was at a very vulnerable point. He acknowledged his priorities and for the first time, he structured his life by putting his priorities first. In the past, he had always squeezed his priorities into whatever time was leftover in his days.

Like Logan, does this loss offer you a chance to restructure your life around the things that truly matter to you?

_____

_____

_____

_____

_____

_____

_____

_____

Many times we make our priorities fit in around the rest of our daily responsibilities. Can you align yourself more with your priorities by restructuring after your loss?

_____

_____

_____

_____

_____

_____

_____

While finding meaning comes with time and hindsight, if we keep our eyes open we are prone to discovering many insights along our grieving path. This Step contains exercises to help you uncover new insights and foster new meaning. This is definitely a Step that you will need to refer to throughout the months and years ahead, as you will gain added perspective with time and reflection.

Learning through Loss

You may want to keep a special page in your journal (or use the designated pages in this *Companion Workbook*) to record the lessons and affirmations you learn throughout your grieving process. Any lesson, no matter how seemingly insignificant, should go on these pages. These pages serve as a reflection that we are moving forward.

This idea originally came from Patricia Ellen and was used in *I Wasn't Ready to Say Goodbye: surviving, coping and healing after the sudden death of a loved one*. Since then, I have used the exercise with many people. You will find examples of this exercise on pages 161-163 of the Grief Steps® book. You can read the lessons I learned in my Closing Note in the Grief Steps® book on pages 209-211.

Use the space below and on the following page to create your own list of lessons.

_____

_____

_____

_____

_____

_____

_____

_____

_____

_____

_____

_____

_____

_____

_____

_____

_____

_____

_____

_____

Questions for Exploring Meaning

The following questions are challenging and there is no need to answer them right away. In fact, this exercise is best a year or so down the road when you've had a bit more time to assimilate your loss. When you are ready, spend some time with these questions. Write about them in your journal. See what surfaces—and how what surfaces—might be the beginning of a new phase of life for you.

Is a change occurring? Could your loss have occurred just when a particular phase of change and growth had been completed for you? Could it be that you are now being catapulted into a greater phase of growth—that in spite of your tremendous loss and disrupted life, a new you, full of vital life force and creativity is ready to emerge (or has already begun to emerge)?

_____

_____

_____

_____

_____

_____

_____

_____

_____

_____

_____

_____

_____

_____

_____

_____

What does the whole picture reveal? Look at your life in totality to this point. Think about your life prior to your loss. Then think about your life now. What lessons did you learn? What lessons can you learn?

_____

_____

_____

_____

_____

_____

Is there a life lesson? Every opportunity, no matter how painful, offers growth if we are strong enough to meet the challenge. What life lesson can this experience teach you? What growth might this experience encourage?

_____

_____

_____

_____

_____

_____

_____

_____

Is this a springboard to something greater? In her book _Don't Let Death Ruin Your Life,_ Jill Brooke examines the link between greatness and loss. She documents many famous, high-achievers who suffered severe loss in their life or at an early age. It is fascinating to see the linkage between loss and achievement in these lives. I highly recommend examining this section of her book.

_____

_____

_____

_____

_____

_____

_____

_____

_____

_____

_____

_____

_____

_____

Sometimes we find meaning by being thankful. We can begin by being thankful for the littlest of things, like making it through the day. As we practice gratitude, it becomes easier and easier to increase our thankfulness. The following exercise can help you explore meaning through gratitude.

Thank You Exercise

As you continue to grow and heal you will eventually discover at least something (no matter how seemingly insignificant) for which you can express gratitude. If the expression is not available to you now, it is probably a temporary condition.

When you are ready, you might want to try this Thank You Exercise. Compared to all other acts, personal and spiritual growth is greatest through the expression of gratitude. No matter how difficult at first, expressing appreciation for some aspect of your loss (no matter how minor) can help make some meaning in the face of tragedy. Acknowledging, in writing, what was empowering and uplifting, will help you retain what was valuable—and to let go of the false belief that you cannot grow or learn after your loss.

_____

_____

_____

_____

_____

_____

_____

_____

_____

_____

_____

_____

_____

_____

_____

_____

_____

_____

_____

_____

_____

_____

Notes:

Step Eight:
Redefining Ourselves

Purpose: To understand the void that has been created by our loss and how that void will change our personal belief system.

◆

"Transformation stems from a shift in perspective…it also means looking at the positives and negatives of one's life and seeing what treasures can be recovered from the rubble." ~ **Patricia Commins, FINDING MOTHER, FINDING MYSELF**

Loss doesn't just affect one area. The shadows of loss affect other aspects of our lives as well, requiring us to examine the emptiness that has been created. When we understand this, we can go about the business of redefining ourselves and filling the emptiness.

As you begin the Step of redefinition, understand that you don't need to know all the answers now. No one will force you or hold "a clock to your head" asking you to redefine yourself over night. Redefinition is a process. It involves soul-searching, courage and rediscovery. It takes time.

Simply stated, the question becomes, "Now what?" After expecting life to take a certain course, it has chosen it's own, far from your plans. Again, take it slow. Choose one thing that you know for certain.

Off the top of your head, write down one thing you know for certain.

_____

_____

_____

_____

_____

_____

_____

Looking at Life Now

After any loss, our life tends to fall into three categories. On the following page, you'll find a worksheet divided into three columns.

(1) What I know for sure... or things that definitely won't change.
(2) Things that definitely will change.
(3) Things that could change—in other words, opportunities that have been created for change.

Begin with column one, filling in those things that you know for sure. For example, if you have always loved to paint, or if you love animals—record those aspects of your identity in this column. These are the stable pieces of your life.

Next, move to column three and record what has definitely changed in your life. If most of your days were spent caring for an aging parent who has now passed, you might right "full time caregiver" in column three. Perhaps you were a very active person who has experienced a physical injury or disability that will change your level of activity. Maybe you loved to travel and did so regularly, but due to a divorce or financial setback, you will not be able to travel as frequently. Record any areas of your life that will undoubtedly change in column three.

Column two is the bridge between what won't change and what will change. Where have opportunities been created? Where is there uncertainty? If you were a wife or husband who has become single, there is a gray area. Will you choose to enter a new relationship? It is not important to have the answer now—just the question. Perhaps there was a hobby you shared with a best friend or romantic interest who has now left your life. The hobby may be painful to continue—but you have a choice as to whether to continue it or not. That type of option would be listed in column two.

This exercise isn't devised to make a neat life-graph that you can follow. The purpose is to have an awareness of what is left of your foundation and to identify opportunities for choice and growth. You will also know where you must rebuild and where important decisions need to be made. Awareness is key. If we live life unaware, life will deal the cards for us. As you work through this exercise, you would do well to keep the Serenity Prayer nearby for easy reference...

God grant me the Serenity
to accept the things I cannot change;
Courage to change the things I can;
and Wisdom to know the difference.
~Reinhold Neibuhr

Areas that definitely won't change:	Areas that definitely will change:	Areas where there are opportunities for change:

The remaining exercises within this chapter will help you uncover more of the opportunities that can be added to your Looking at Life Now Worksheet. The point of this exercise is to look at life from all different angles and to become aware of what your life is—and isn't.

Hope Note: This is a future that has been "handed to us," we have not chosen it. It would be easy to fall victim to this turn of events, but by choosing actions to help with our healing, we become "emotional heroes" not victims.

Exercises for Understanding What We Have Lost

The Void: To truly acknowledge our grief, we must examine the void that has surfaced. Write about the changes you have experienced because of your loss. What areas of your life are incomplete? If you have experienced the ending of a relationship, you might have lost physical contentment in your life, closeness, love. If you have lost a parent, you may experience the void of trusted wisdom or a mentor. If you have moved, you might experience the loss of a home or community. If your job was your loss, you might be facing financial insecurity. Explore your specific void in detail. Try writing about what you have lost and what the loss means to you.

_____

_____

_____

_____

_____

_____

_____

Likewise, loss often affects more than one area of our life. For example, if we have lost our significant other our spirituality may be affected because we question God. If it was a breakup our self-esteem and self-worth may plummet. We may not take care of ourselves physically. We may find our homes to be lonely instead of welcoming. We may stop engaging in hobbies we once enjoyed. Although the loss was in one area—our relationship area—it affects a broad spectrum within our lives.

In the spaces below, write about how your loss has affected the following areas of your life:

Spirituality

_____

_____

_____
_____
_____
_____
_____

Self-esteem and Mental-health

_____
_____
_____
_____
_____
_____
_____

Physical health

_____
_____
_____
_____
_____
_____
_____

Work life

_____
_____
_____
_____
_____
_____
_____

Home life

_____
_____
_____
_____

_____

_____

_____

Hobbies

_____

_____

_____

_____

_____

_____

_____

Relationships

_____

_____

_____

_____

_____

_____

_____

Special interests

_____

_____

_____

_____

_____

_____

_____

_____

> *When we understand the void that has been left,*
> *we can go about the business of redefining ourselves.*

Another Angle

Think of your life as a house. The person that you are is the "roof" of the house. Your life experiences and the people that you know are the beams that brace the roof. What beams have crumbled because of your loss? How does that affect the roof? What beams are still there, but might be bent or crooked because your experience has challenged them? Record your thoughts and feelings below.

_____

_____

_____

_____

_____

_____

_____

_____

_____

_____

_____

_____

_____

_____

_____

_____

_____

_____

_____

_____

This is similar to the Void Exercise but offers another perspective. Often, when we examine experiences through different lenses, we uncover more of their truth.

Examine Your Expectations

When we look at our expectations, we can see the depth of our loss and the hole that has been created in our life. Again, this Redefining Step helps us to understand the void so that we can then understand what is needed to fill it. Try answering the following questions about expectations:

What did you expect from this part of your life?

_____

_____

_____

_____

_____

_____

_____

How do you feel life has been unjust to you?

_____

_____

_____

_____

_____

_____

_____

What did you look forward to that has been taken away?

_____

_____

_____

_____

_____

_____

_____

> *We need to examine our expectations and how they have been broken. Then we need to form new expectations based on our current reality.*

Exercises for Understanding What We Have Left

What Do I Love? When immersed in our sadness and feelings of loss, we sometimes forget about the wonderful things our life has held for us over the years. Try to create a list of 25 things that you love to do, or be a part of. Aim to include things that you can still engage in, despite your loss. Perhaps walking in nature, watching funny movies, baking, traveling, photography, a craft project—list as many things as possible. As you emerge from your grief, use this list to gravitate toward activities that will bring you enjoyment.

There is a slogan commonly used in A.A. groups… "Act as if…" Basically, the slogan means that we act as we wish to be, and by continually doing that we become who we want to be. Try implementing this activity by engaging in activities that have brought you joy in the past.

What My Experience Has Left Me

When we lose someone or something important to us, it is not unusual to have a sense that one was rejected or abandoned in some way. When you are feeling this searing pain and anger of abandonment, it is even more difficult to consider that your pain may be transformed into something meaningful, or that an end of a relationship (even through death) can be in any way beneficial to your growth. It can be. Especially if you were dependent on the other person for good feelings about yourself. Now is the time to look within and to affirm yourself as a person of value. It is also the time to remember and replay any positive messages you heard from your significant other before they died. Write some of these positive messages in the space provided below.

_____

_____

_____

_____

_____

_____

_____

_____

_____

_____

_____

_____

_____

_____

_____

_____

_____

_____

_____

_____

_____

_____

_____

_____

_____

_____

Step Nine: Living with Our Loss

Purpose: To integrate our newly discovered meaning into our day-to-day lives and to move forward despite our loss.

♦

"...every day, grief puts on a new face."
~ **Wendy Feiereisen**

If we truly think about it, in its most basic sense, much of who we are is composed of the reflections of those we meet and the experiences we have gone through. Have you ever noticed that you pick up the lingo or tonal inflections of those you spend time with? Have you found yourself with mannerisms or similar interests of close friends? Perhaps, just as much as we are individuals, we are also composed of the traits and qualities we inherit from interactions with others.

In her book, *Don't Let Death Ruin Your Life*, author Jill Brooke writes, "No one that we have ever loved can totally disappear from our lives. Our loved ones live on in our gestures, our mannerisms, our beliefs and our feelings." The same can be said for any loss we have faced.

At this point in our grief journey, we have faced many of the difficult emotions that come with loss. We are at the point at which we realize life does go on—and somehow, we need to reunite with life and move forward.

Make a List

Try making a list of the qualities that you valued in your loved one. Or, if your loss was not a person, list the qualities that you valued from your life experience. Add to the list for a week or two until you have at least 25 qualities that were represented by your loss.

Once you have 25 qualities, review your list, looking for qualities that you could incorporate or improve in your current life. Write your discoveries below.

_____
_____
_____
_____
_____
_____
_____
_____
_____
_____
_____
_____
_____
_____
_____
_____
_____
_____

Transfer the discoveries that resonate the most with you onto index cards and place the cards where you will see them often. You may also want to keep a journal, recording how you implement these qualities each day. Your journal may take the form of regular entries, or you can write letters to your lost loved one, sharing how you are honoring their memory. You can do a similar activity with your loved one's interests and beliefs. What did they honor? What did they believe in? What purpose did they contribute to, or hope to contribute to? Write about how you can keep those visions alive as you move forward.

_____
_____
_____
_____
_____
_____
_____
_____

Tell Stories that Incorporate Your Loss

As you move forward, share how this experience touched your life and what you learned. Share your funny memories. Share your sad memories. Even though you have experienced loss, you can keep fond memories alive through the stories that you share. Recall one story, happy or sad, and record it below.

_____
_____
_____
_____
_____
_____
_____
_____
_____
_____
_____
_____
_____
_____
_____
_____
_____
_____
_____
_____
_____
_____
_____
_____
_____
_____
_____

Reflections

If your loss is a person or relationship, look for the ways it has reflected into who you are. It is through these reflections we can honor our loved one, and carry their traits into the future with us. These thoughts, traits, memories and mannerisms will also serve as a link to our loved ones. What positive characteristics or qualities do you possess that show the reflections of your loss in your life?

_____

_____

_____

_____

_____

_____

_____

_____

_____

_____

_____

_____

_____

_____

_____

_____

_____

_____

_____

_____

_____

_____

_____

_____

_____

_____

Rituals

Read the section on rituals from the *Grief Steps®* book, pages 189-196. Then take an evening this week and think about what rituals feel good to you. What would help you to honor and create space for your loss? Choose one ritual to begin and choose a date. Write about your choice below. Then schedule your ritual on your calendar and follow through. Healing involves many steps—let this be one of them.

_____

_____

_____

_____

_____

_____

_____

_____

_____

_____

_____

_____

_____

_____

_____

How to Create Your Own Ritual

Creating your own ritual may seem like a difficult task, but it doesn't have to be. To begin, ask yourself what you are trying to remember or celebrate.

_____

_____

_____

_____

For many, a ritual on the anniversary of the loss is valuable. Others find they'd like to honor another memorable day. If you have lost someone through death, their birthday might be a day for reflection. There are no limits to rituals. You can have one each season of the year, or one annually or every other year. Think about the purpose of your ritual as you decide on frequency.

What date and frequency comes to mind as you think through the ritual process?

_____

_____

_____

_____

_____

Do you want the ritual to be just for yourself or do you want to share it with others. You may find that having a group of friends engage in the ritual is helpful. Others like this time to explore their emotions by themselves.

_____

_____

_____

_____

_____

Where you should conduct your ritual is the next question to answer. There may be a special place that you associate with your loss. You may want to stay close to home or you may wish to travel overseas. Again, keep your purpose in mind as you choose your location.

_____

_____

_____

_____

_____

Using the ideas for rituals from the Grief Steps® book and your answers to the proceeding questions, write a summary of the ritual you would like to implement.

_____

_____

_____

_____

_____

_____

_____

_____

_____

_____

Notes:

Step Ten:
Accepting Our New Life

Purpose: To take responsibility that life is ours to be lived to the fullest.

◆

"What the caterpillar calls the end of the world, the master calls a butterfly." ~ **Richard Bach**

One might think that after exploring all these steps, this would become the easiest chapter to write, and the easiest chapter to read. After all, we have gone through so many exercises, stages and explorations together. However, I have found this to be the most difficult chapter to write. Perhaps that is because of the power of change. Throughout this book we have dealt with understanding our crisis and assimilating our loss into our life. At this point, we are on the cusp of emerging from the grip of grief and coming out "the other side" into new territory. Such significant change often elicits anxiety and a bit of fear. It is at this point we can be so tempted to turn back toward our grief, rather than move on. It can be easy to convince ourselves that we can't really move forward, and sentence ourselves to stay "stuck." That is the challenge we both face here... how do I give you some parting words to retain the strength that has brought you this far, and how do you hold onto that strength after you close the cover of this workbook?

If you haven't joined us already, this would be a perfect time to join the online support group that I monitor. In this safe and secure e-mail group, grievers share their journeys, trials and triumphs. To join, simply go to www.griefsteps.com and click on the Online Group link. We would love to support you as you move forward. As wonderful as the group is, I want to give you more as you "graduate" from this phase of grief and move forward. You have worked hard to get here. I have tried hard to help guide you. While you have learned much already, there are more lessons I would like you to carry forward.

We can only rejoin society and accept and affirm life as we are ready. We must complete all the Grief Steps® to truly lead a complete life. It is not a process that we can force, but it also is not a process we should hide from. It is not a process that will happen automatically; we must take a step forward to meet life and trust life, with a willing heart. This will not happen all at once. It is like learning to walk. Our first steps are likely to be wobbly, unsteady, and we will likely fall. With a support group around us, we can get up and try again—slowly building our courage until we can walk forward and meet life with open arms.

Defining Priorities and Stepping Toward Fulfillment

If loss brings one disguised gift, it is the gift of evaluation, reflection and resultant change. We often go about our days on autopilot, moving moment-to-moment without much thought. When loss lands in our lap, the disruption creates a pause where we are given the opportunity to reflect, re-evaluate and rebuild. One of the best ways to honor our experience is to use it as a stepping stone to be more true to our heart's desires—and to be more present in day-to-day life. We learn to turn off that autopilot and we quit letting the moments wash together. We take control of directing our lives toward our true desires.

Uncovering those true desires and deciding what or how to change takes time, thought, reflection and healing. The following questions can help you take a look at your life priorities and focus on what truly matters to you now.

1. What are the most important elements of life for me?
   (Often you'll discover a common thread in your choices.)

_____

_____

_____

_____

_____

_____

_____

_____

_____

2. Based on what I've learned, how would I describe a fulfilling life for myself?

_____

_____

_____

_____

_____

_____
_____
_____
_____
_____

3. What steps can I take today to move toward that fulfilling life?

_____
_____
_____
_____
_____
_____
_____
_____
_____

4. What steps can I take tomorrow?

_____
_____
_____
_____
_____
_____
_____
_____
_____

"Little by little, just as the deaf, the blind, the handicapped develop with time an extra sense to balance disability, so the bereaved, the widowed, will find new strength, new vision, born of the very pain and loneliness which seem, at first, impossible to master."
~ Daphne Du Maurier,
The Rebecca Notebook

Accepting Change

When we experience loss, we make something very difficult and very sad—very real. If we honor our loss, speak of our loss, and incorporate it into our life (which is healthy, and our right to do) it means that those who are around us will be reminded that loss is very real—and can happen to anyone at any time.

Many people are ill-equipped with the emotions and strength to face that reality. That is why our friends and family want us to "get back to normal"—they want us to get back to where they don't have to look at that reality in the eye. But that is a place we cannot go back to—at least not if we choose the healthy path. For this reason, we will shed many friends or notice friendships change. Although I don't know what experience Joni Mitchell was facing, the lyrics from her song, "Clouds" are very powerful:

And now my friends are acting strange
they shake their heads,
and tell me that I've changed
well there's something lost
and something gained
in living life this way...

I've looked at life from both sides now,
from up above, from near and far
and still somehow
it's life's illusions I recall,
I really don't know life at all.

What feelings do these lyrics elicit from you?

_____

_____

_____

_____

_____

_____

_____

_____

_____

An Exercise in Hope

During our darkest days, we often spend much of our time focusing on our sadness and our loss. Developing a sense of hope, no matter how small, can be a wonderful way to lift our spirits and remind us of all the reasons to move forward.

Sarah Ban Breathnach in her bestselling book, *Simple Abundance: A Daybook of Comfort and Joy*, advocates the use of a gratitude journal. She sites this as "a tool that could change the quality of your life beyond belief." We usually think of starting gratitude exercises at a hopeful point in life—such as a New Year Resolution. However, it is in our darkest hour that we need these exercises the most. The gratitude journal that Breathnach suggests is a special notebook where each and every day, we record five things for which we are thankful. Some days the list will be easier to make than others. Some days, your list might include things like, "I'm grateful this day has ended!" The value lies in looking for experiences for which we can be grateful.

Recognizing the positives in our lives is especially important when we are engulfed in dark times. We often focus so heavily on our loss and what isn't going right, that we can't see any of the good things. For the first few months, it will be extremely difficult to find the positives, but after that initial time period, we need to begin looking again—no matter how simple these positives might be. Your list might include something as basic as "I was able to get out of bed today." What's important is that we be open to the fact that there are positives. By recognizing them, we attract more positives to our life.

For one week, keep your own gratitude list by recording five experiences or events for which you are grateful in the spaces below.

Monday

_____

_____

_____

_____

_____

Tuesday

_____

_____

_____

_____

_____

Wednesday

_____

_____

_____

_____

_____

Thursday

_____

_____

_____

_____

_____

Friday

_____

_____

_____

_____

_____

Saturday

_____

_____

_____

_____

_____

Sunday

_____

_____

_____

_____

_____

At the end of the week, use the following page to write what you learned from this exercise. It will likely become an activity you will want to continue!

Calming Exercise

Stress, anxiety, sadness, depression—these emotions can leave us knotted inside. Practicing deep breathing exercises can help you to relax and unwind your wound-up-emotions. The following exercises will help calm you during trying times.

Place one hand on your abdomen. As you inhale, you want to feel the movement in your abdomen, not in your chest. Inhale for the count of ten, then exhale for the count of ten. Repeat this ten to fifteen times for deeper relaxation.

To relax your whole body, lay down in a quiet place. Breathe deeply, slowly inhaling and exhaling. Beginning with your left leg, clench your muscles as tightly as you can for the count of three. Then relax them. Do the same with the right leg, left arm and right arm. Then move up your body tightening and relaxing your pelvis, then stomach, then chest, then shoulders, then neck and lastly facial muscles. When you have completed this exercise you should feel extremely calm and peaceful. Visualize an ocean beach or other calming scene to deepen the relaxed feelings.

Record your experience with the calming exercise in the space provided below.

_____
_____
_____
_____
_____
_____
_____
_____
_____
_____
_____
_____
_____
_____
_____
_____
_____
_____

In Closing...

And so, after all is said and done, we end up here— in the final pages of this workbook. First, congratulate yourself for your commitment to healing. I read somewhere that over 90% of books are never read past page 20. Reading these words shows your commitment to moving forward. I hope you took the time to thoughtfully complete the exercises. If not, or if you skipped a few, go back and work through the workbook (and book) again. Your time spent in healing will be well worth it. In the meantime, I hope you will join our online group at www.griefsteps.com. I am on the boards there at least once a week… I look forward to meeting you there. In the meantime remember that you have an inner strength. Even if you do not realize it, you are an "emotional hero".

"What the caterpillar calls the end of the world,
the master calls a butterfly."
~ Richard Bach

"To leave the world a bit better, whether by a healthy child, a garden path, or a redeemed social condition; to know even one life has breathed easier because you have lived. This is to have succeeded."
~ **Ralph Waldo Emerson**

Bibliography

Adrienne, Carol. The Purpose of Your Life Experiential Guide. William Morrow, 1999.

Akner, Lois F. Whitney, Catherine (contributor). *How to Survive The Loss of a Parent: A Guide for Adults.* Quill, 1994.

Albertson, Sandy. *Endings and Beginnings.* Random House, 1980.

American Association of Retired Persons Brochure, *Frequently asked Questions by the Widowed.*

American Association of Retired Persons Brochure, *On Being Alone.*

American Association of Retired Persons web site article, "Common Reactions to Loss."

Blair, Pamela and Noel, Brook. *I Wasn't Ready to Say Goodbye: Surviving, Coping and Healing After the Sudden Death of a Loved One.* Champion Press Ltd, 2001.

Bowlby, John. *Loss: Sadness and Depression.* Harpercollins, 1980,

Bozarth, Alla Renee. *A Journey Through Grief: Specific Help to Get You Through the Most Difficult Stages of Grief.* Hazelden, 1994.

Bramblett, John. *When Goodbye Is Forever : Learning to Live Again After the Loss of a Child.* Ballantine, 1997

Breathnach, Sarah Ban. *Simple Abundance: A Daybook of Comfort and Joy.* New York: Warner, 1995.

Brooke, Jill. *Don't Let Death Ruin Your Life: A Practical Guide to Reclaiming Happiness After the Death of a Loved One.* E.P. Dutton, 2001.

Childs-Gowell, Elaine. *Good Grief Rituals: Tools for Healing.* Station Hill, 1992.

Coffin, Margaret M. *Death in Early America.* Thomas Nelson, 1976.

Collins, Judy. *Singing Lessons : A Memoir of Love, Loss, Hope, and Healing.* Pocket Books, 1998.

Cournos, Francine. *City of One.* Plume, 2000.

Curry, Cathleen L. *When Your Spouse Dies: A Concise and Practical Source of Help and Advice.* Ave Maria Press, 1990.

Deits, Bob. *Life After Loss : A Personal Guide Dealing With Death, Divorce, Job Change and Relocation.* Fisher, 1992.

Du Maurier, Daphne. *The Rebecca Notebook and Other Memories.* Book Sales, 1983.

Doka, Kenneth J (editor). Kenneth, Kola J. (editor). Hospice Foundation of America. *Living With Grief After Sudden Loss : Suicide Homicide Accident Heart Attack Stroke.* Taylor and Francis, 1996.

Edelman, Hope. *Motherless Daughters: the legacy of loss.* Delta, 1995.

Ericsson, Stephanie. *Companion Through the Darkness : Inner Dialogues on Grief.* Harper Perennial Library, 1993.

Fulber, Marta. *Grief Expressed: When a Mate Dies.* Lifeword, 1997.

Fine, Carla. *No Time to Say Goodbye : Surviving the Suicide of a Loved One.* Main Street Books, 1999.

"Final Details." Brochure by The American Association of Retired Persons.

Fitzgerald, Helen. *The Mourning Handbook : The Most Comprehensive Resource Offering Practical and Compassionate Advice on Coping With All Aspects of Death and Dying.* Fireside, 1995.

Friedman, Russell and John W. James. *The Grief Recovery Handbook : The Action Program for Moving Beyond Death Divorce, and Other Losses.* Harpercollins, 1998.

Freud, Sigmund. From a letter to Ludwig Binswanger who had lost a son.

"Forgotten Mourners." The Journal News, July 29, 1999.

Fumia, Molly. *Safe Passage : Words to Help the Grieving Hold Fast and Let Go.* Conaris Press, 1992.

Gibran, Kahlil. *The Prophet.* Random House.

Ginsburg, Genevieve Davis. *Widow to Widow: thoughtful practical ideas for rebuilding your life.* Fisher Books, 1995.

Grey, John. Gootman, Marilyn E. *When a Friend Dies: A Book for Teens About Grieving and Healing.* Free Spirit, 1994.

Gordeeva, Ekaterina. Switft, E.M. (contributor). *My Sergei: A Love Story.* Warner, 1997.
Grollman, Earl A. *Living When A Loved One Has Died.* Beacon Press, 1995.

Golden, Tom LCSW. "A Family Ritual for the Year Anniversary." Tom Golden Grief Column.

Goldman, Linda. *Breaking the Silence: A guide to help children with complicated grief.* Western Psychological Services.

Gootman, Marilyn. *When a Friend Dies: a book for teens about grieving and healing.* Free Spirit Publishing, 1994.

Goulston, Mark MD and Philip Goldberg. *Get Out of Your Own Way.* Perigee, 1996.

Halifax, Joan. *The Fruitful Darkness: Reconnecting With the Body of the Earth.* Harper San Francisco, 1994.

Harris, Maxine. *The Loss That is Forever: The Lifelong Impact of the Early Death of a Mother to Father.* Plume, 1996.

Hays, Edward M. *Prayers for a Planetary Pilgrim: A Personal Manual for Prayer and Ritual.* Forest of Peace Books, 1998.

Heegaard, Marge Eaton. *Coping with Death and Grief.* Lerner Publications, 1990.

Henricks, Gay. *The Learning to Love Yourself Workbook.* Prentice Hall, 1992.

Johnson, Elizabeth A. *As Someone Dies: A Handbook for the Living.* Hay House, 1995.

Kennedy, Alexandra. *Losing a Parent: Passage to a New Way of Living.* Harper San Francisco, 1991.

Kolf, June Cezra. *How Can I Help? : How to Support Someone Who Is Grieving.* Fisher Books, 1999.

Kubler-Ross, M.D., Elisabeth. *On Children and Death: How children and their parents can and do cope with death.* Simon and Schuster, 1997.

Kushner, Harold S. *When Bad Things Happen to Good People.* Avon, 1994.

L'Engle, Madeleine. *Sold into Egypt : Joseph's Journey into Human Being.* Harold Shaw, 1989.

Lerner, Harriet. *The Dance of Anger : A Woman's Guide to Changing the Patterns of Intimate Relationships.* HarperCollins, 1997.

Livingston M.D, Gordon. *Only Spring: On Mourning the Death of My Son.* Marlowe & Company, 1999.

Marshall, Fiona. *Losing A Parent: A Personal Guide to Coping With That Special Grief That Comes With Losing a Parent.* Fisher Books, 1993.

Matsakis, Aphrodite. *Trust After Trauma : A Guide to Relationships for Survivors and Those Who Love Them.* New Harbinger Publications, 1998.

Matsakis, Aphrodite. *I Can't Get Over It: A handbook for trauma survivors.* New Harbinger Publications, 1996.

Mabe, Juliet. *Words to Comfort, Words to Heal: Poems and Meditations for Those Who Grieve.*

Marx, Richard. Wengerhoff Davidson, Susan. *Facing the Ultimate Loss: Confronting the Death of a Child.* Champion Press, Ltd. 2003.

McWade, Micki. *Daily Meditations for Surviving a Breakup, Separation or Divorce.* Champion Press Ltd, 2002. *Getting Up, Getting Over, Getting On: A 12 Step Guide to Divorce Recovery.* Champion Press, Ltd., 2000.

Mechner, Vicki. *Healing Journeys: The Power of Rubenfield Synergy.* Omniquest, 1998.

Melrose, Andrea LaSonder (editor). *Nine Visions: a book of fantasies.* Seabury Press, 1983.

Miller Ph.D., Jack. *Healing our Losses: A Journal for Working Through your Grief.* Resource Publications.

Mitchard, Jacquelyn. *The Deep End of the Ocean.* Penguin, 1999.

Noel, Brook with Art Klein. *The Single Parent Resource.* Champion Press, 1998.

Nouwen, Henri J. *Reaching Out : The Three Movements of the Spiritual Life.* Image Books, 1986.

Overbeck, Buz and Joanie Overbeck. "Where Life Surrounds Death." Adapted from Helping Children Cope with Loss.

O'Neil, Anne-Marie; Schneider, Karen S. and Alex Tresnowski. "Starting Over." *People* magazine, October 4, 1999. p 125.

Prend, Ashley Davis. *Transcending Loss: Understanding the Lifelong Impact of Grief and How to Make It Meaningful.* Berkely, 1997.

Rando, Therese A. *Treatment of Complicated Mourning.* Research Press, 1993.

Rando Ph.D, Therese A. *How to Go on Living When Someone You Love Dies.* Bantam, 1991.

Rilke, Rainer Maria. *Letters to a Young Poet.* WW Norton, 1994.

Rosof, Barbara D. *The Worst Loss: How Families Heal from the Death of a Child.* Henry Holt, 1995.

Sachs, Judith with Lendon H. Smith. *Nature's Prozac : Natural Therapies and Techniques to Rid Yourself of Anxiety, Depression, Panic Attacks & Stress.* Prentice Hall, 1998.

Sanders, Dr. Catherine M. *Surviving Grief.* John Wiley, 1992.

Schiff, Harriet Sarnoff. *The Bereaved Parent.* Viking, 1978.

Shaw, Eva. *What to Do When A Loved One Dies: A Practical and Compassionate Guide to Dealing With Death on Life's Terms.* Dickens Press, 1994.

Sheehy, Gail. *Passages.* Bantam, 1984.

Staudacher, Carol. *A Time to Grieve : Meditations for Healing After the Death of a Loved One.* Harper San Francisco, 1994.

Staudacher, Carol. *Beyond Grief : A Guide for Recovering from the Death of a Loved One.* New Harbinger Publications, 1987.

Stearn, Ellen Sue. *Living With Loss : Meditations for Grieving Widows (Days of Healing, Days of Change).* Bantam, 1995.

Stoltz PhD, Paul G. *Adversity Quotient : Turning Obstacles into Opportunities.* John Wiley & Sons, 1999.

Tatelbaum, Judy. *The Courage to Grieve.* HarperCollins, 1984.

Temes, Dr. Roberta. *Living With an Empty Chair : A Guide Through Grief.* New Horizon, 1992.

Viorst, Judith. *Necessary Losses : The Loves, Illusions, Dependencies, and Impossible Expectations That All of Us Have to Give Up in Order to Grow.* Fireside, 1998.

Westberg, Granger E. *Good Grief.* Fortress Press, 1971.

Zarda, Dan and Marcia Woodaard. *Forever Remembered.* Compendium, 1997.

Zunin M.D., Leornard M. and Hilary Stanton Zunin. *The Art of Condolence.* Harper Perennial Library, 1992.

A Guide for Those Helping Others with Grief

(photocopy and give to close friends and loved ones)

Don't try to find the magic words or formula to eliminate the pain. Nothing can erase or minimize the painful tragedy your friend or loved one is facing. Your primary role at this time is simply to "be there." Don't worry about what to say or do, just be a presence that the person can lean on when needed.

Don't try to minimize or make the person feel better. When we care about someone, we hate to see them in pain. Often we'll say things like, "I know how you feel," or "perhaps, it was for the best," in order to minimize their hurt. While this can work in some instances, it never works with grief.

Help with responsibilities. Even though a life has stopped, life doesn't. One of the best ways to help is to run errands, prepare food, take care of the kids, do laundry and help with the simplest of maintenance.

Don't expect the person to reach out to you. Many people say, "call me if there is anything I can do." At this stage, the person who is grieving will be overwhelmed at the simple thought of picking up a phone. If you are close to this person, simply stop over and begin to help. People need this but don't think to ask. There are many people that will be with you during the good times—but few that are there in life's darkest hour.

Talk through decisions. While working through the grief process many bereaved people report difficulty with decision making. Be a sounding board for your friend or loved one and help them think through decisions.

Don't be afraid to say the name of the deceased. Those who have lost someone usually speak of them often, and believe it or not, need to hear the deceased's name and stories. In fact, many grievers welcome this.

Excerpted from "I Wasn't Ready to Say Good-bye: a guide for surviving, coping and healing after the sudden death of a loved ones" by Brook Noel and Pamela D. Blair, Ph.D. (Champion Press, 2000)

Remember that time does not heal all wounds. Your friend or loved one will change because of what has happened. Everyone grieves differently. Some will be "fine" and then experience their true grief a year later, others grieve immediately. There are no timetables, no rules—be patient.

Remind the bereaved to take care of themselves. Eating, resting and self-care are all difficult tasks when besieged by the taxing emotions of grief. You can help by keeping the house stocked with healthy foods that are already prepared or easy-to-prepare. Help with the laundry. Take over some errands so the bereaved can rest. However, do not push the bereaved to do things they may not be ready for. Many grievers say, "I wish they would just follow my lead." While it may be upsetting to see the bereaved withdrawing from people and activities—it is normal. They will rejoin as they are ready.

Avoid judging. Don't tell the person how to react or handle their emotions or situation. Simply let him/her know that you support their decisions and will help in any way possible.

Share a Meal. Invite the bereaved over regularly to share a meal or take a meal to their home since meal times can be especially lonely. Consider inviting the bereaved out on important dates like the one-month anniversary of the death, the deceased's birthday, etc.

Make a list of everything that needs to be done with the bereaved. This could include everything from bill paying to plant watering. Prioritize these by importance. Help the bereaved complete as many tasks as possible. If there are many responsibilities, find one or more additional friends to support you.

Make a personal commitment to help the one grieving get through this. After a death, many friendships change or disintegrate. People don't know how to relate to the one who is grieving, or they get tired of being around someone who is sad. Vow to see your friend or loved one through this, to be their anchor in their darkest hour.

Excerpted from "I Wasn't Ready to Say Good-bye: a guide for surviving, coping and healing after the sudden death of a loved ones" by Brook Noel and Pamela D. Blair, Ph.D. (Champion Press, 2000)

Appendix B: Other Resources to Help You Heal

Facing the Ultimate Loss: Coping with the Death of a Child by Robert J. Marx and Susan Davidson... After experiencing the loss of his own son and working with hundreds of individuals, Rabbi Marx worked with psychologist Susan Davidson to create a guide for coping with the passage of losing a child.

Paperback Book $14.95
Hardcover Book $23.95

GriefSteps: 10 Steps to Recover, Regroup and Rebuild After Any Life Loss by Brook Noel...Bestselling author Brook Noel worked with hundreds of people to discover what allows some people to rebuild after loss while others don't.

Price: $14.95

I Wasn't Ready to Say Goodbye: surviving coping and healing after the sudden death of a loved one by Brook Noel & Pamela D. Blair, Ph.D... this bestselling book has become an anchor for thousands who are navigating grief's journey after the unexpected death of someone they love.

Paperback Book $14.95

I Wasn't Ready to Say Goodbye: surviving coping and healing after the sudden death of a loved one – Companion Workbook
This workbook helps grievers explore their feelings and emotions and cope with grief's grip.

Paperback Book $18.95

Grief Steps.Com Offering 24/7 Support

Grief Steps is a program created by best-selling author Brook Noel, to reach out and provide support to the many people experiencing loss in their lives. She created www.griefsteps.com to offer 24/7, free internet support to anyone needing support through loss.

Joining is Free and Simple

Simply log onto <u>www.griefsteps.com</u> You will find support chats, support e-mail groups, a reading room, a free newsletter and other support services. Membership is free and the support is there for you—as little or as much as you need.

Appendix C: Online Support Classes, Groups and Resources

Take a step toward healing with interactive, online courses led by best-selling author Brook Noel

How do the classes work?

Its easy to get started with a GriefSteps class. Simply enroll in the class of your choice at www.griefsteps.com We offer a wide variety of classes ranging in price from $19 to $129.

What do I get with my class?

1. Once you enroll, you'll receive a welcome packet that will contain directions for the classes.

2. Each class has "assignments" that you can turn in for comments from Brook Noel.

3. Some classes include weekly chats or other designated chat times hosted by Brook Noel.

*Participate in chats, message boards and assignments is optional.

Healing Exercises – Part One

In this interactive, online course, you'll complete 10 different exercises that help you move forward through grief and resolve open issues. The exercises can be completed again and again after the class to further your healing. Brook Noel will comment on work you choose to turn in and encourage you in your journey.

Class length – 6 weeks   Cost $49

Now What? Living After Loss

This class offers a solid foundation for anyone wondering how to go on after loss. You'll learn what to expect physically and emotionally and how to take your first steps toward healing.

Class length – 3 weeks   Cost $19

Rituals to Honor Your Loved One

Rituals are a wonderful way to keep the memory of your loved one with you. This class will introduce you to different types of rituals and guide you in creating one of your own.

Class length – 4 weeks   Cost $29

When Will the Pain End?
Working through Unresolved Grief

Throughout this 10 week course, you'll learn about the different stages of grief and how to recognize which of your life losses have not been grieved completely. You'll learn exercises and tactics to heal and work through unresolved grief, which are the most common causes of sadness and depression. This is the perfect class for anyone who is having difficulty moving forward after a life loss.

Class length – 10 weeks   Cost $99

The Healing Journey: Writing through Grief

In this writing-intensive class, you'll learn how to write the story of your loss and discover its meaning. You'll create a record of your cherished memories and discover how your loved one is still in your life today. When you complete this class you'll have a very special chronicle of you and your loved ones relationship.

Class length – 12 weeks   Cost $129

How to Create Your Own Support Group

In this class you will be given assignments that will lead to the creation of your own support group by the completion of the course. You'll decide what type of support group you want to start (online or in-person), create materials to help spread the word and learn how to successfully guide your support group meetings.

Class length – 8 weeks   Cost $79

Basic Strategies and Exercises for Healing

In this interactive, online course, you'll complete 4 different exercises that can help you on your grief journey. You'll also learn what to expect on your journey and strategies for coping.

Class length – 3 weeks   Cost $19

Take a step toward healing.
Enroll today at www.griefsteps.com

Appendix D: *Exploring Grief Questionnaire*

Take this questionnaire as instructed in the beginning of the workbook. When you complete the workbook, complete the questionnaire again to check your progress.

1. My loss occurred within the last 3 months. ____ Y ____ N

2. I feel numb, like I can't believe this has happened. ____ Y ____ N

3. Sometimes I feel like everything is happening in slow motion. ____ Y ____ N

4. If someone asked "How do you feel?" I could identify my emotions. ____ Y ____ N

5. I have felt intense sadness. ____ Y ____ N

6. I have felt intense anger. ____ Y ____ N

7. I understand what happened. ____ Y ____ N

8. My mind is clear and I have quit thinking about this situation
   constantly. ____ Y ____ N

9. I have given myself the time and space to grieve as needed. ____ Y ____ N

10. If the loss occurred over several months ago, I have continued to cry
    occasionally since that time. ____ Y ____ N

11. I talk openly about my loss. ____ Y ____ N

12. Despite my sadness, I have been able to see why the loss
    happened. ____ Y ____ N

13. I have reached out to others in a similar situation and offered my help. ____ Y ____ N

14. I understand what has happened and do not think about my loss
    constantly. ____ Y ____ N

15. I have identified the void left by my loss and have begun to
    take action to fill it. _____ Y _____ N

16. I have continued communicating, in a healthy way, with my friends. _____ Y _____ N

17. I have maintained (or returned to) the hobbies I was engaged
    in before my loss. _____ Y _____ N

18. I feel bitter inside. _____ Y _____ N

19. I feel angry inside. _____ Y _____ N

*If you have a religious background, please answer questions 20-23. If not, please go
to question 24.*

20. I have quit going to church. _____ Y _____ N

21. I have quit praying. _____ Y _____ N

22. I question how God could let this happen. _____ Y _____ N

23. I don't feel my faith community understands what I am
    going through. _____ Y _____ N

24. I have created rituals to honor my loss. _____ Y _____ N

25. I can think about my loss without extreme sadness. _____ Y _____ N

26. I am engaging in new hobbies and trying new things. _____ Y _____ N

27. I have made new friends. _____ Y _____ N

28. I have returned to work. _____ Y _____ N

29. I feel hope more often than I feel hopelessness. _____ Y _____ N

30. I see a purpose for my life. _____ Y _____ N

Appendix E: Suggested Reading

General books for adults

A Time to Grieve: Meditations for Healing After the Death of a Loved One by Carol Staudacher, Harper SanFrancisco, 1994—365 daily readings offer comfort, insight and hope. This book is written specifically for people after the death of a loved one, however it is appropriate for anyone who still copes with the effects of a loss of any kind. A great gift for yourself or a grieving friend.

Beyond Grief by Carol Staudacher, New Harbinger Publications, 1987—This book is about understanding and then coping with loss, with clearly stated suggestions for each part of the grieving process. Written both for the bereaved and the helping professional, it combines supportive personal stories with a step-by-step approach to recovery. *Beyond Grief* acknowledges the path, reassures and counsels. Includes guidelines to create support groups and guidelines for helping others. It says to the grieving person: you are not alone, you can get through the pain, and there is a path back to feeling alive again.

Companion Through Darkness: Inner Dialogues on Grief by Stephanie Ericsson, Harperperennial Library, 1993—As a result of her own experience with many kinds of loss, the author offers an intimate, touching guide for those in grief. The book combines excerpts from her own diary writings with brief essays.

Complicated Losses, Difficult Deaths: A Practical Guide for Working Through Grief by Roslyn A. Karaban, Ph.D., Resource Publications 1999—Written by a pastoral counselor, certified grief therapist and death educator, the book deals with losses that are more difficult to cope with than others: suicide, sudden loss, the death of a child and murders among others---losses that evoke grief reactions and symptoms that are more intense and last longer than "ordinary" grief.

Dreams that Help You Mourn by Lois Lindsey Hendricks. Resource Publications, 1997--This book will put you in the company of other mourners and their dreams. You'll learn that dreaming after losing a loved one is absolutely normal. In fact, it's the soul's way of mourning. The book will help you take better advantage of the healing power of your dreams.

I Can't Get Over It: A handbook for trauma survivors by Aphrodite Matsakis, New Harbinger Publications, Inc., 1996—Explains how post-traumatic stress disorder (PTSD) affects survivors of a variety of traumas including disasters, rape, crime and violence. Addresses the survivor directly and helps them self-diagnose to then get appropriate treatment. Includes a variety of techniques and self-help suggestions for safe recovery.

In Memoriam: A practical guide to planning a memorial service by Amanda Bennett and Terence B. Foley, Fireside Books, 1997--Written in an easy-to-read format, this book provides a full range of options to help you choose music, arrange flowers, select a format, prepare a eulogy and invite speakers and offers a wide range of selected appropriate readings.

Life After Loss: A personal guide dealing with death, divorce, job change and relocation by Bob Deits, Fisher Books, 1992—Provides skills for healthy recovery, including how to cry, how to write a goodbye letter, how to deal with emotions and how to cope.

Moving Beyond Grief: Lessons from those who have lived through sorrow by Ruth Sissom, Discovery House, 1994—A religiously oriented book offering stories of persons who have learned to cope with grief and trauma.

The Courage to Grieve by Judy Tatelbaum—This book covers many aspects of grief and resolution. Divided into five sections, it explores the grief experience and creative recovery.

The Dream Messenger: How Dreams of the Departed Bring Healing Gifts by Patricia Garfield. The author writes about the distinctive patterns that she discovered in her research of over 400 dreams. These include images of a journey, dream gifts from the departed, a "soul animal" whose characteristics are associated with the departed person, and images of a "veil" or boundary that separates the living the from the dead. She emphasizes that such dreams are an esential part of the healing process around mourning, providing comfort to the bereaved.

What to Do When a Loved One Dies: A practical and compassionate guide to dealing with death on life's terms, by Eva Shaw, Dickens Press, 1994—Presents excellent guidelines describing what to do when a death occurs. It has an extensive listing of support groups, resources and other sources of help. The approach is extremely detailed and includes sections on dealing with catastrophic deaths.

With Those Who Grieve: Twenty grief survivors share their stories of loss, pain and hope—by Kay Soder-Alderfer, Lion Publishing, 1994—Describes the healing process of grief and its effects, as well as how to find and offer help. The stories of grief cross the lifespan.

Words to Comfort, Words to Heal: Poems and Meditations for those Who Grieve compiled by Juliet Mabey, Oneworld Publications, 1998—This lovely book would make a nice gift to give another or to give yourself. It features works drawn from poets, writers, philosophers and sacred literature. An inspirational anthology that celebrates lives that have ended and offers consolation to those left behind.

Books about grief recovery

Grief's Courageous Journey: A Workbook by Sandi Caplan and Gordon Lang, New Harbinger Publications, 1995—Grieving the loss of a loved one is an intensely personal process. This workbook takes the hand of those who are left behind and guides them, at their own pace, along the path of their own healing journey. It provides a compassionate program for coping with day-to-day life and accepting the changes in yourself and others. Guided by a sequence of journaling exercises and suggestions for creating healing personal rituals, you can use the workbook to tell the story of your relationship with the person who died, grieve your loss and safely remember the past. You will also learn techniques for redefining your present life and re-creating your sense of future. The book includes a comprehensive ten-session facilitator's guide for creating a grief support group in your community.

Healing our Losses: A Journal for Working Through Your Grief by Jack Miller, Ph.D., Resource Publications—The author shares experiences of loss in his own life and will guide you to record your memories, thoughts, and feelings about loss in your life. Journaling may be done alone or in a group setting.

Healing the Heart; Letting Go; Therapeutic Stories for Trauma and Stress; Stories to Heal the Grieving Heart (AUDIO TAPES), N. Davis, 1995, 6178 Oxon Hill Rd., Suite 306, Oxon Hill, MD, (301) 567-9297—These audio tapes contain collections of therapeutic stories designed to ease the process of grieving, explain stages of grief, address the intuitive side of the mind and help the listener find what he/she needs within the self. Visual imagery and relaxation exercises are also included.

Managing Traumatic Stress through Art: Drawing from the center by Barry M. Cohen, Mary-Michola Barnes and Anita B. Rankin, The Sidran Press, 1995—Provides step-by-step art experiences designed to help the reader understand, manage and transform the after effects of trauma. Written in a practical, useful style that shows the ways in which art making and writing can assist one's healing from severe trauma.

The Grief Recovery Handbook by John W. James & Russell Friedman (Revised Edition), HarperCollins, 1998— Drawing from their own histories, as well as from others, the authors illustrate what grief is and how it is possible to recover and regain energy and spontaneity. Based on a proven program, this book offers grievers specific actions needed to complete the grieving process and accept loss.

Books for grieving men

Griefquest : Men Coping With Loss by Robert Miller, St. Mary's Press, 1999—*GriefQuest* is a book of meditations written for men and the women who love and care about them. This book, written by other men, helps make sense out of the unique challenges that grief and loss force on men today.

Grief Therapy for Men by Linus Mundy, Abbey Press, 1998—This little book acknowledges the uniqueness of male grief and offers men real permission to grieve. It gives a host of practical suggestions for healthy male grief—what to do, what not to do, when to act boldly and when to just "be."

Men & Grief: a guide for men surviving the death of a loved one by Carol Staudacher, New Harbinger Publications, 1991— *Men & Grief* is the first book to look in depth at the unique patterns of male bereavement. Based on extensive interviews with male survivors, it describes the four characteristics of male grief, explains the forces that shape and influence male grief and provides step-by-step help for the male survivor.

When Men Grieve : Why Men Grieve Differently and How You Can Help by Elizabeth Levang, Fairview, 1998-- Insightful text on the unique characteristics of men's grief and how they face loss. Includes poetry and strategies for partners, friends and relatives.

Books about the loss of a friend

Grieving the Death of a Friend by Harold Ivan Smith, Augsburg Fortress Publications, 1996--The death of a friend is one of the most significant but unrecognized experiences of grief in American culture. This unique new book moves with, rather than against, the natural grief process by exploring its many aspects--the friending, the passing, the burying, the mourning, the remembering and the reconciling.

When a Friend Dies: A book for teens about grieving and healing by Marilyn E. Gootman, Ed.D., 1994, Free Spirit Publishing, Minneapolis, MN—A small, powerful book whose author has seen her own children suffer from the death of a friend. She knows first hand what teenagers go through when another teen dies. Very easy to read, some of the questions dealt with include: How long will this last? Is it wrong to go to parties and have fun? How can I find a counselor or therapist? What is normal?

Books about helping someone who is grieving

The Art of Condolence by Leonard M Zunin, M.D & Hilary Stanton Zunin, Harperperrenial Library, 1992—Offers specific and wise advice for responding to another's grief. Discusses what to write, what to say, and what to do.

When Your Friend's Child Dies: A Guide to Being a Thoughtful and Caring Friend by Julane Grant, Angel Hugs Publishing, 1998—A simply written, straight-forward book that will tell you what to say and do when you have a friend whose child has died. And, just as important, Chapter 1 tells you what not to say and why. An early reader described this book as a "slap-in-the-face wake-up call." After reading this book you will know how to comfort a parent who has lost a child, even ten years later.

You Can Help Someone Who's Grieving : A How-To Healing Handbook by Victoria Frigo, Penguin, 1996—A practical resource that deals with such issues as what to say and not to say after someone dies, how long the grieving period lasts and its many stages, how to write sympathy notes, and how to handle holidays and anniversaries.

Books about the loss of a child

A Broken Heart Still Beats: When Your Child Dies edited by Anne McCracken and Mary Semel, Hazelden, 1998—Edited by two mothers who have lost a child, this book combines articles and excerpts—some fiction, some nonfiction—that featured the death of a child. A brief introduction to each chapter, describes a different stage of the grieving process and how it affected their lives.

After the Darkest Hour the Sun Will Shine Again : A Parent's Guide to Coping With the Loss of a Child by Elizabeth Mehren, 1997—This inspiring guide to coping with the loss of a child combines the author's own story with the experiences and wisdom of others who have gone through this tragedy.

After the Death of a Child : Living With Loss Through the Years by Ann K. Finkbeiner, John Hopkins University Press, 1998—Drawing on her own experience with losing a child, an inspirational self-help guide for parents examines the continuing love parents feel for their child, ways to preserve the bond and strategies for coping with loss.

Recovering from the Loss of a Child by Katherine Fair Donnelley, Berkley Publishing Group, 1994—The death of a child is one of life's cruelest blows. This comforting book offers bereaved parents, siblings, and others inspiring firsthand accounts from people who have survived this heartbreaking experience. In addition to healing advice, the book illustrates how such deaths affect family relationships.

The Worst Loss: How families heal from the death of a child by Barbara D. Rosof, Henry Holt & Co., Inc., 1994—The death of a child overwhelms many people. This book describes the losses that the death of a child brings to parents and siblings as well as potential PTSD reactions and work of grief. A very thorough and wise book. One of our favorite books on the topic.

When Goodbye Is Forever : Learning to Live Again After the Loss of a Child by John Bramblett , Ballantine, 1991—In 1985, John and Mairi Bramblett's youngest child, two-year-old Christopher, died in an accident, leaving them and their three older children devastated by shock and grief. Four months later, John began writing this deeply moving and honest story of how he and his family coped with the nearly unbearable pain of losing their son. *When Goodbye is Forever* walks us along the author's path to acceptance and recovery, taking us through the first hours and days of the tragedy, the painful but necessary first outings, and such occasions as Christopher's birthday, and the anniversary of his death. Mairi and the children share their responses to the tragedy as well, showing us the effect such a tragedy can have on the whole family.

Books for children and teens and their caregivers

A Taste of Blackberries by Doris B. Smith, Harpercollins Juvenil Books, 1992 (8-9 years)—The author conveys the experience and feelings of an eight-year-old boy whose best friend Jamie dies unexpectedly. The boy and his family, along with Jamie's family, deal with the myriad of questions and feelings engendered by this unexpected event.

Bart Speaks out: Breaking the Silence on Suicide (ages 4-12), by Linda Goldman, MS, Western Psychological Services, Los Angeles, CA—Bart, a lovable terrier, misses his owner Charlie, who has just died. But Bart's grief is complicated by the silence that surrounds Charlie's, death. Sad and puzzled, Bart gradually comes to understand that Charlie has committed suicide. This workbook will give children an opportunity to explore suicide openly, to resolve their grief by breaking through the barriers of shame and secrecy that typically cloud this subject. Workbook exercises dispel myths about suicide, provide age-appropriate facts and explanations, and show children how to express their feelings.

Beat the Turtle Drum by Constance C. Greene, 1976, The Viking Press, NY (10-14 years)—In this touching story, the effect of the sudden death of an 11-year-old child on her older sister and parents is told with warmth and sensitivity.

Bereaved Children and Teens: A Support Guide for Parents and Professionals by Earl A. Grollman, Beacon Press, 1996—Explores the ways that parents and professionals can help young people cope with grief. Topics covered include what children can understand about death at different ages, the special problems of grieving teenagers, how to explain Protestant, Catholic, or Jewish beliefs about death in ways that children can understand, and more.

Breaking the Silence: A guide to help children with complicated grief by Linda Goldman, Western Psychological Services, Los Angeles, CA—Designed for both mental health professionals and parents, this book provides specific ideas and techniques to use in working with children who have suffered psychologyical trauma from violence, homicide, suicide or other traumas. Explains how to break the silence and then how to help children recover.

Coping with Death and Grief by Marge Eaton Heegaard, Lerner Publications, 1990—Includes stories about young people, grades 3-6, who deal with grief. Provides facts about death that are developmentally based.

Don't Despair on Thursdays! (ages 4-12) by Adolph Moser, Ed.D., Western Psychological Services, Los Angeles, CA— This gentle book lets children know that it's normal to grieve in response to loss and that grief may last more than a few days or weeks. Offers practical suggestions that children can use, day by day, to cope with the emotional pain they feel. Young readers will be comforted by the reassuring text and colorful illustrations.

Goodbye Rune (ages 5-11), by Marit Kaldhol and Wenche Oyen, Western Psychological Services, Los Angeles, CA— Rune and Sara are best friends, until the day that Rune accidentally drowns. This is a sensitive account of a child's first experience with death, Sara asks her parents endless questions, and their patient answers help her come to terms with the loss of someone special. She comes to realize that, through her memories, Rune will always be with her. Explores death and grief in terms children can understand.

Helping Bereaved Children, edited by Nancy Boyd Webb, DSW, Western Psychological Services, 1999—This book for therapists includes therapeutic interventions for children who have suffered a loss. Individual chapters focus on such topics as, death of a grandparent, father or mother, accidental sibling death, suicide of mother, violent death of both parents, traumatic death of a friend, sudden death of a teacher, and more.

It happened to me: A story for child victims of crime or trauma,
Something bad happened: A story for children who have felt the impact of crime or trauma and *All my feelings: A story for children who have felt the impact of crime or trauma* by D. W. Alexander, 1992, Huntington, NY, Bureau for At-risk Youth— These coloring/workbooks are designed for early elementary school students. They identify the various components of PTSD and help with healing.

Life & Loss: A guide to help grieving children (Preschool through teen), by Linda Goldman, Western Psychological Services, Los Angeles, CA—Helpful information using photographs, children's drawings, essays, anecdotes and other simple techniques. Gives all the tools you need to help children through the grief process. Includes, how to recognize various kinds of loss, avoid blocked feelings, the four psychological tasks of grief, and how to commemorate loss among other topics. Offers a guide to community and national support groups and a list of materials addressing specific kinds of loss.

Lifetimes: A beautiful way to explain death to children by Bryan Mellonie & Robert Ingpen, Bantam Doubleday, 1987— A moving picture book for children of all ages that lets us explain life and death in a sensitive, beautiful way. With large color illustrations, it tells us that dying is as much a part of living as being born.

Part of Me Died, Too: Stories of creative survival among bereaved children and teenagers by Virginia Lynn Fry, 1995, Dutton Children's Books, NY—Eleven true stories about young people who experienced the loss of family members or friends in a variety of ways including, murder, suicide and accident. Includes writings, drawings, farewell projects, rituals and other creative activities to help children bring their feelings out into the open.

Straight Talk About Death for Teenagers: How to Cope with Losing Someone You Love by Earl A.Grollman, Beacon Press, Boston, MA, 1993 (13-19 years)—With reassurance and compassion, Grollman explains normal reactions to the shock of death, the impact of grief on relationships, dealing with pain, funerals, and much more. Includes a place for readers to record their memories.

Talking About Death: A Dialogue between Parent and Child by Earl A. Grollman, Beacon Press, 1991—How do you explain the loss of a loved one to a child? This compassionate guide for adults and children to read together features an illustrated read-along story, answers to questions children ask about death, and comprehensive lists of resources and organizations that can help. Helpful for children from preschool to preteen.

The Good Mourning Game by Nicholas J. Bisenius, PhD and Michele Norris, MSW, Western Psychological Services, Los Angeles, CA—Using an artistically designed game board, this resource is a wonderful therapy tool for children who've suffered a loss. The board illustrates nature's basic cycle, which, like the grief cycle, moves from stormy intensity to relative calm. It can be played by a therapist and one to three children in usually about 45 minutes.

The Grieving Child: a parents guide by Helen Fitzgerald. Fireside, 1992—Compassionate advice for helping a child cope with the death of a loved one. Also addresses visiting the seriously ill, using age-appropriate language, funerals, and more.

The way I feel: A story for teens coping with crime or trauma
It happened in Autumn: A story for teens coping with a loved one's homicide by D. W. Alexander, 1993, Huntington, NY, Bureau for At-risk Youth—These short books which include space for completing exercises, are part of a 6-volume series designed for teens exposed to crime and trauma.

What on Earth do you do When Someone Dies? (ages 5-10) by Trevor Romain, Western Psychological Services, Los Angeles, CA—Someone you love dies, and your whole world changes. Written to and for kids, this little book offers comfort and reassurance to children who've lost a loved one. It answers questions children often ask such as, Why? What next? Is it my fault? What's a funeral? It is still okay to have fun? Will I ever feel better? Includes a list of practical coping strategies.

When Something Terrible Happens: Children can learn to cope with grief (ages 6-12) When Someone Very Special Dies: Children can learn to cope with grief by Marge Eaton Heegaard, Woodland press, 1992—These two books teach basic concepts of death and help children, through their workbook format, to express feelings and increase coping skills. Children use their own personal stories to complete the pages as they draw events and their accompanying feelings.

Books about the death of a mate

How to Go On Living When Someone You Love Dies by Therese A. Rando, Ph.D., 1988, New York, Lexington Books—Includes suggestions for ways to deal with sudden or anticipated death. Offers self-help techniques to work on unfinished business, take care of the self and when to get help from others. Leads you through the painful but necessary process of grieving and helps you find the best way for yourself. Offers guidance to help you move into your new life without forgetting your treasured past.

Grief Expressed: When a Mate Dies by Marta Felber. Lifeword, 1997—This compassionate workbook guides you through the process of grieving the death of a mate. Sensitive writing and practical exercises help you to address issues such as loneliness, building a support system, managing sleepless nights, finances, self-nurturing and much more. The author has drawn from her own counseling background, as well as her self-healing after the death of her husband.

Widow to Widow: Thoughtful practical ideas for rebuilding your life by Genevieve Davis Ginsburg, M.S., 1995, Fisher Books—The author writes from her own experience as a widow and therapist. The book is frankly honest and attempts to dispel myths, disputes the rules and encourages the widow to begin her new life in her own way and time.

When Your Spouse Dies: A Concise and practical source of help and advice by Cathleen L. Curry, Ave Maria Press, 1990—This short book deals with a variety of practical topics within a spiritual framework. Includes topics such as advice on loneliness and sexuality, financial priorities and planning and good health practices, among others.

Living with Loss: Meditations for Grieving Widows by Ellen Sue Stern, 1995, Dell Publishing, NY—This book, small enough to fit in a purse, is full of supportive and empowering reflections. This daily companion is designed to help you cope today, cherish yesterday and thrive tomorrow.

Books about losing a parent

How to Survive the Loss of a Parent: A guide for adults by Lois F. Akner, Catherine Whitney, 1994, William Morrow & Co.—Therapist and author, Lois Akner, explains why the loss of a parent is different from other losses and using examples from her experience, shows how it is possible to work through the grief.

Losing a Parent: Passage to a New Way of Living by Alexandra Kennedy, Harper San Francisco, 1991—Based on the author's personal experience, she writes on topics such as keeping a journal, saying goodbye, tending to your wounds and the "living parent within you."

Losing a Parent: A personal guide to coping with that special grief that comes with losing a parent by Fiona Marshall, 1993, Fisher Books—Offers comforting and inspiring advice for helping one cope with the different and difficult effects of loss. The author includes insightful and practical strategies to use in dealing with the surviving parent and other family members. Looks at the impact of the sudden death of a parent as well as terminal illness. It also includes suggestions on how to locate help and inheritance issues.

Mid-Life Orphan: Facing Life's Changes Now That Your Parents Are Gone by Jane Brooks. Berkely Books, 1999—Many mid-life orphans feel isolated, even abandoned, when their parents dies, but they also learn how to cope and extract life lessons from their experience. This book focuses on a loss that has been a fact of life for centuries, but has moved to the forefront as baby boomers, who represent 1/3 of the U.S. population, are forced to deal with this age of loss.

Motherless Daughters: The legacy of loss by Hope Edelman, Delta, 1995—Includes stories of women whose mothers have died early in their lives and how the absence of a mother shapes one's identity.

The Loss That is Forever: The Lifelong Impact of the Early Death of a Mother or Father by Maxine Harris, Ph.D., Plume, 1996—Explores the impact that early loss of a parent has on every aspect of development. Who one becomes, how one loves, how one parents, and what one believes about the world, are all shaped by the experience of this loss. Provides comfort and guidance for coping and shows how the human spirit can survive and master this loss.

Order Form

Item #	Description	Qty,	Price	Subtotal

Order total: _____

WI Residents Please Add 5.6 % sales tax: _____

($3.95 for the first book, $1 for each additional) Shipping: _____

Total: _____

SHIP TO INFORMATION:

Name _____

Address _____

_____

_____

Phone

E-mail Address:

Method of Payment:

☐ Check   ☐ MasterCard

☐ Visa

_____   _____

Credit Card #   *Exp. Date*

_____

Signature

Send this order form to:

Champion Press, Ltd
4308 Blueberry Road
Fredonia, WI 53021
www.griefsteps.com